IN SEARCH OF AMERICAN PLACE-NAME ORIGINS

IN SEARCH OF AMERICAN PLACE-NAME ORIGINS

Clues to Understanding Our Nation's Past and Present

Abraham Resnick

iUniverse, Inc.
Bloomington

IN SEARCH OF AMERICAN PLACE-NAME ORIGINS
Clues to Understanding Our Nation's Past and Present

iUniverse books may be ordered through booksellers or by contacting:

iUniverse
1663 Liberty Drive
Bloomington, IN 47403
www.iuniverse.com
1-800-Authors (1-800-288-4677)

Because of the dynamic nature of the Internet, any web addresses or links contained in this book may have changed since publication and may no longer be valid. The views expressed in this work are solely those of the author and do not necessarily reflect the views of the publisher, and the publisher hereby disclaims any responsibility for them.

Any people depicted in stock imagery provided by Thinkstock are models, and such images are being used for illustrative purposes only.

Certain stock imagery © Thinkstock.

ISBN: 978-1-4697-5805-3 (sc)
ISBN: 978-1-4697-5807-7 (e)

Printed in the United States of America

iUniverse rev. date: 02/29/2012

For Saul Scott

Fond remembrances of decades past – and in recognition of his exceptional ability to:

Catch balls	Current event analyze
Calculate math	Clothing manufacture
Celestial navigate	Connect with people

With much gratitude and appreciation to Margaret Sapienza for her very valuable assistance in bringing this book to fruition.

Perfect choices: Gila in Arizona   Gilda in Florida

CATEGORIES OF PLACE-NAME ORIGINS

Additional Information

Continued on pages 94-95

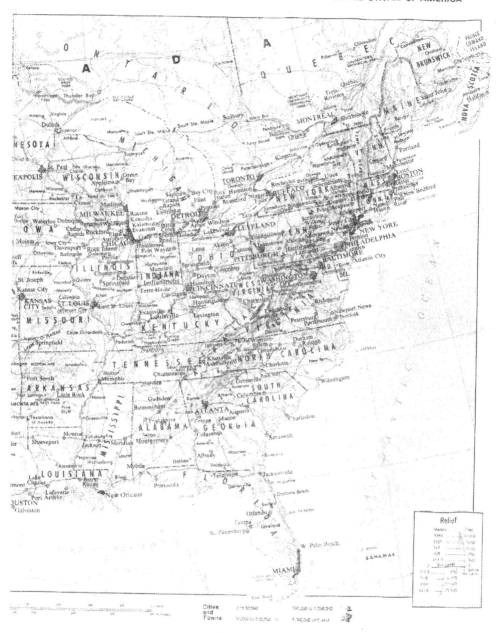

Introduction

The coverage of the content in this book is generally contiguous or conterminous, limiting its information to all of the United States, exclusive of Alaska and Hawaiian place-names.

Names give a place identity and image. They tell us about its site and topographical features and something about its past. Collectively they are like characters in a regional story.

When the definition or creation of a word is unknown or unclear referring to a dictionary can prove to be most useful. On the other hand, should information about the origin of a place be required, an atlas or gazetteer would be of little help. Finding out about how or why a certain geographical place derived its name can be fairly elusive. Often facts about a place-name's beginnings can be obscure or remain a mystery. For the more inquisitive minded individual interested in learning how a place-name may have evolved, an array of guidelines and examples are cited in this book. They are designed to facilitate a researcher's quest for informational clues that should provide insights into our nation's past, its land and people.

A name is a word or a combination of words by which a person, place or thing is known. Names have been used for thousands of years as a means of identification and designation. They help in the clarification process. Places, like people, have a broad assortment of name types. Searching for and analyzing place name origins can convey fascinating and enriching ways geography, history and language are interrelated. The study of place-name origins is called Toponomy. It is a valuable tool utilized by social science investigators and others interested in learning about the early roots and reasons for the naming of a place. With rare exception, generally all names mean something and have had some sort of origin. Most name interpretations or explanations are valid, however, some names may have come about through imagined stories, enhanced by local color, told over a period of time.

In the United States most Americans tend to be unaware of the origins or meanings of how or why their communities or other places receive their names. Place-names are usually taken for granted. This is unfortunate. Even for the moderately curious person, a visit to a local library, historical society, or check of street names can reveal much about a place's past or site and situation.

The examination of old maps and property deeds and the interviewing of elderly folks can prove to be a valuable primary source for name determinations. So too can a review of church records and copies of a region's early newspapers. The archives of county record buildings are usually helpful as well.

An underlying intent of this book is to foster an increased consciousness of one's surroundings and to be inquisitive about the factors that may have contributed to local and area place-namings. Were the names selected commemorative of an event, recognition of a past incident, in honor of a noteworthy person, in remembrance of a founder, or have some national, ethnic or foreign linguistic basis? Could they have stemmed from a literary reference, a geographic feature, or as is often the case, have an American Indian meaning? Hopefully the reader will become more mindful and ever-alert to clues that may lead to speculation and critical thinking of what a particular place-name may tell us. Making a mere assumption or guess as to the reason for a place's original name can prove to be a gratifying educational challenge, especially when traveling with other passengers during automobile trips along roads that post multiple name signs along the way. The activity can serve to negate trip-boredom and stimulate an enlightening discussion.

It has often been asked, "what's in a name?" Plenty. Actually names can be quite revealing. A family name like Baker, Mason, Carpenter, Miller, Smith or Seaman may suggest the occupation of one's forbearers. Or names like Sheffield, Palermo, Salzburg, Hollander, English and Berlin could imply that an ancestor once lived in that region. They may have special connotations about one's ancestry. Though these examples may only be suppositions, reflecting on their possibilities could arouse interest, pride and knowledge about a person's lineage and heritage. Learning about place-name origins can be equally rewarding.

Some place-name origin discoveries may be easy to discern, and hardly challenging, when drawing conclusions about their labelings. It may be obvious to those who remember early American history that the Hudson River was named in honor of the English navigator and explorer Henry Hudson. Likewise one could readily connect the naming of all geographic Delaware designations as a tribute to Sir Thomas West, Lord De La Warr, the first governor of Virginia colony. Uncovering the origins of Chicago and Cincinnati will require a more thorough research.

The former name was derived from an Algonquian term meaning "onion place" by the American Indian tribe living in the area in the late sixteen hundreds. The latter city's name came about when local leaders decided to pay homage to an organization of officers formed after the Revolutionary War, named in honor of Cincinnatus, a former soldier of early Rome.

Another class of names are those of locality, which are often derived from places of generic names as Hill, Dale, Cliff, Lake, Woods or Rivers for example. Many are descriptive in nature. The geographic features are readily found on just about every physical-political map of the United States.

Most place-name origins, on the other hand tend to be less than obvious and demand a fairly thorough inquiry, or even a research of the literature, in order to discover the meaning of or how a given place was named. The investigation will usually reveal special man to man and man to land relationships that will, in all probability, provide meaningful reflections about our nation's past.

American place-names stem from a collection of topics and categories. Twelve different categories of place-name origins are featured in this book. Each classification is treated as a separate chapter. In addition, each chapter highlights a descriptive overview narrating significant historical and geographic themes and factors that have had a role in determining the naming of certain locales in the Unites States. The distinctive circumstances discussed will help the reader foster appreciations and understandings about the interconnections between the naming of specific places and their beginnings.

A diverse group of representative place-names that conform with aspects mentioned in each of the subject categories are listed randomly. The examples selected tend to illustrate and reinforce the concept that place-name designations, along with the probable explanations of their meanings, have deep-rooted sources derived from earlier generations of Americans and their activities in a new land and open frontier.

Though the names of some place-names and their origins may have, over the years, changed, been altered or evolved since their early identities became known, the name listings provided are for the most part accurate and valid.

Note: The place-names treated in this book pertain to those political divisions that are contiguous and have a common boundary within the United States. They include all the states but Alaska and Hawaii.

It was therefore appropriate to resort to a long-established publication entitled <u>Bulletin 197, United States Geological Survey, The Origin of Certain Place-Names in The United States</u>, by Henry Gannett, Geographer, published in Washington, D.C. by the Government Printing Office, in 1902.

Bulletin 197 had a compilation giving the origin of some ten thousand place-names in the United States. Numerous additional sources were also relied on to cross-reference and verify many of the place-name origins culled from Bulletin 197.

Four additional sources were examined in order to underscore the founding and tracing of a host of site place-names and the originations of each mentioned.

1. **Place-names Of The World**; Origins and Meanings for over 5,000 Natural Features, Countries, Capitals Territories, Cities and Historic Sites, by Adrian Room, McFarland & Co., Jefferson, N.C. and London 1997.

2. **American Place-names**; A concise and Selective Dictionary for the Continental United States of America, by George R. Stewart, Oxford University Press, New York, 1970.

3. **Goode's World Atlas**; 16th Edition, published by Rand McNally & Company, Chicago, 1984, was also relied on for its glossary of foreign geographical terms as they interrelated with significant aspects of the origins of American words and place-names. The etymology and listings of the topical categories usually illustrate the development of a particular word or words. They may often reveal much about the description of a site's natural flora and fauna.

4. **Penguin Reference, The New York Times Almanac, 2008**; Wright, John W., Editor, New York, NY, 2007

I.

~

NAMES OF HISTORICAL EVENTS AND PERSONS OF NOTE

P rimarily historical names take on three forms of recognition. Incident names are bestowed upon places for a particular event occurring there or at a nearby area, for a place named by a landlord or settler, and in honor of, and in commemoration of extraordinary contributions made by a distinguished person or groups of people.

Influential officials, in their name recognitions, frequently relied on their own knowledge of history. National origins and heritages, as well as biblical figures and storied accounts mentioned in the testaments were used as well. Designating place-names for American heroes was not to be overlooked. Neither were crucial battles with native tribesmen and the outcomes of their conflicts. Furthermore, American value themes that stressed liberty, freedom and democracy became imbedded in the nomenclature naming processes.

Early on American explorers paved the way for settlements upon its uncharted lands. Scouts and soldiers were in the vanguard of newly discovered sites. Impromptu names were bestowed upon nameless landscapes. Throughout the early years of United States history many exploratory journeys were made over formidable terrains and upon streams and rivers. Places were quickly identified based on early impressions, including the nearby fauna and flora. Certain locations were aptly described and plotted on schematic maps for later travelers to uncover in traversing of the continents.

The westward expansion from 1800 to 1860 proved to be vital for place naming initiatives. Throughout that period the United States acquired vast regions including the Louisiana Purchase, the Oregon Country, and ceded territory from Mexico. The nation also obtained miles of territory called the Gadsden Purchase (1853) which ultimately became part of New Mexico and Arizona, with place labels having a Spanish resonance throughout the area.

The acquisitions were compliant with the introduction of a new policy executed by the American government labeled "Manifest Destiny". This was a concept, or idea, that the nation was destined to own the entire lands from the Atlantic Ocean to the Pacific Ocean. The settlements with such a huge land "empire" called for the new, or renaming, of places. This became essential as current events unfolded into the far reaches of the vast region. Cartographers had their work cut out for them by the need for providing maps that were valid and up-to-date. Their references hold true to this day. Their efforts still persist as they are charged with assigning heretofore anonymous names to places.

The historical events that took place during the early parts of the 17th, 18th and 19th centuries centered around disputes between nations over territorial claims, colonization, deep-seated culture clashes and their quests for independence from their respective mother countries. New England had become the "cradle of democracy."

The 13 original colonies were predominantly Anglo-Saxon in character. Pockets of Dutch, Swedish, German, Scotch-Irish and French speaking enclaves held on to their old world cultures. The Spanish settlers dotted the southwest and managed to locate missions all along the Pacific Coast of California. Each group ultimately assimilated into an American culture, yet frequently retaining their heritage, backgrounds and places of origin when citing appropriate appellations for their "homogenized" areas.

As the United States developed a diverse group of individuals made their marks upon the country. Specific places where they demonstrated acts of bravery, leadership, political actions and inventiveness have been memorialized with their identifications on maps. Political divisions and other geographic entities bear their banners of honor, reflecting past contributions to America's story.

A collection of distinguished persons received testimonials in the form of having places named after them. Examples are: Patrick Henry (Patriot), Henry Clay (Congressman), Daniel Webster (Statesman), Robert Fulton (Inventor), Daniel Boone (frontiersman) and Oliver Hazard Perry (Commodore). Though of lesser renown, they have left a lasting effect on America's memory.

EXAMPLES OF SPECIFIC PLACE-NAME ORIGINS

Historical Events and Persons of Note

1. **EAGLE, WV 38.10N – 81.20W**

   Bird of prey of the falcon family. Its likeness is used as a symbol, or emblem of the United States. It is noted for its strength, size, and keenness of vision. At least 12 places have the name Eagle. They include rivers, lakes, passes, and towns.

2. **WASHINGTON D.C., 38.50N – 77.00W**

   At least 14 place-names bear the name of the most heroic figure in American history. In the midst of a heavy snowstorm on Christmas night 1776, George Washington and his army crossed the Delaware River and in a surprise attack defeated the Hessian troops (mercenaries who served in the British army) at Trenton, N.J. The victory there turned the tide in favor of the colonial forces.

3. **DONNER PASS, NV TO CA 39.32N – 119.49W; 40.20N – 112.07W**

> A lake and mountainous pass in the 7,017 ft. Sierra Nevada range between Reno, N.V. and the gold resources beyond. In 1846 – 1847 a party of gold prospectors died when a huge snowstorm, lasting for weeks, closed the pass preventing rescuers from reaching the site where 47 out of 87 perished from the cold and starvation. Some of their remains showed that cannibalism (human beings who eat human flesh) took place out of desperation.

4. **VICKSBURG, M.S., 32.20N – 90.50W**

> It is historically famous as a site of one of the most decisive military campaigns of the American Civil War. It was captured by General Grant. Founded by the Rev. Newitt Vick, a minister in 1814, becoming the town of Vicksburg in 1825.

5. **LIBERTY ISLAND, N.Y., 40.40N – 73.58W**

> The famous Statue of Liberty is located on a small island in New York harbor. The 305 ft. high statue was a gift from France on the 100th anniversary of American independence. Nearby is situated Ellis Island, where millions of immigrants were processed prior to entry into the United States.

6. **GETTYSBURG, P.A., 38.50N – 77.5W**

> Scene of Lincoln's renown address delivered November 19, 1863, at the dedication of the cemetery where the remains of 45,000 soldiers fell during the most significant Union victory during the Civil War.

7. **LEWIS AND CLARK, O.R., 46.13N – 124.04W**

> In recognition of the expedition to the Pacific Ocean by Meriwether Lewis and William Clark during the winter of 1805 – 1806. A river in Oregon and a county in Montana are named for them.

8. INDEPENDENCE, M.O., 39.06N – 94.26W

Encompassing patriotic and idealistic themes, commemorating the signing of the Declaration of Independence, are borne by 27 places, among them are Kansas, Ohio, Oregon and Nevada, besides Missouri. Since that day, the U.S. was no longer under the control of the British and they became politically free.

9. VERRAZANO-NARROWS BRIDGE, N.Y.

This is the name of the two-deck bridge built between Staten Island and Brooklyn, New York. It is thought to carry the greatest number of vehicles annually across the waterway below, and probably is the busiest in the world. It is named for the Italian explorer of the east coast, Giovanni da Verrazano.

10. COUNCIL BLUFFS, I.A., 41.16N – 95.53W

This place, like 5 similar named, denotes that some kind of council took place there. The meetings selected bluffs, a butte, a crest or grove for the negotiations between whites and Indians usually over peace negotiations. The Creeks and other tribes used such sites for the performance of colorful ceremonies.

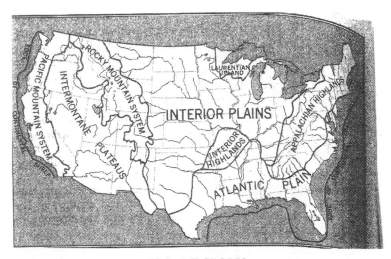

U.S. REGIONS

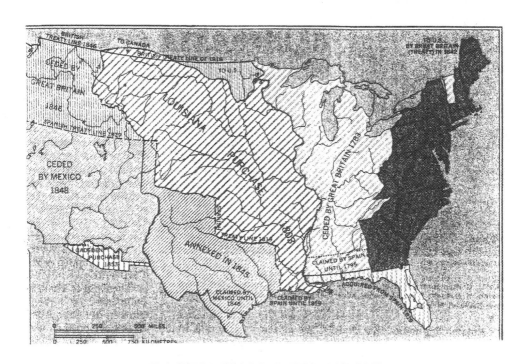

U.S. TERRITORIAL EXPANSIONS

II.

~

GEOGRAPHIC FEATURES AS DETERMINERS OF PLACE-NAMES

Geography is the descriptive science dealing with the surface of the earth. It is considered a major underlying contributor to past and current events. It has been compared to a stage in which the script is enhanced by a backdrop of scenery, upon which actors play different roles.

The real setting of a place often takes on words that may include its geographic configuration. The shape of a site can readily dictate the name of a particular location, especially when it interrelates with water bodies and land features. A place may have been named by an original person dwelling on the land or by cultivating its soil, fishing its waters, grazing its animals upon the open plains, or by mining its mountains. First inhabitants' impressions may leave a lasting indelible imprint upon a geographical entity, with appropriate titles conferred.

Pioneers encountering new topography were quick to label their findings. Their map making featured names that often included diverse references to natural elements and human responses. Additionally, name givers relied on visual observations of landscapes, elevation, fauna and flora, and other elements of the natural environment when applying titles to places.

"Geographic Determinism" is a term or concept used to help understand the ways natural terrains and water bodies have influenced and impacted our lives, past and present. Well over a hundred of these terms or expressions can be located on a political (man-made) or physical (natural) map of the United States. Each geographic feature bears an identifiable name associated with it.

Rivers, lakes and coastal regions can determine navigational routes for ships and boats. Aircraft pilots seek favorable weather conditions in their flight plans. Mountains tend to serve as barriers to the surface movement of goods and people. They may determine the weather, either on the windward (rainy) or leeward (dry) sides, thus determining how people live and crops grow. Dwellings on plains, piedmonts, plateaus and high elevations can attract various kinds of human activity. Minerals are usually imbedded in hill country. Each map feature and accompanying name can reveal much about interrelationships between man and land.

A sampling of geographic features and their accompanying place-names underscore typical disclosures about "human geography". They may include such terms as Lake Michigan, Colorado Springs, Edwards Plateau, Rocky Mountains and Chesapeake Bay. In the language of maps geographic components may also suggest a type of activity that tend to be universally found amongst each landscape, such as Great Salt Lake Desert, Cape Cod, Cedar Rapids, Gulf of Mexico, Long Island Sound, Green Mountains, Potomac River and Long Beach.

1. **The Great Basin** region of the United States is an extremely large area located between the Sierra Nevada and Rocky Mountains. Altitudes there range from 280 feet below sea level to 13,000 foot peaks. The area's climate, soil, water irrigation and natural resources available have made it an attractive place for farming and mining, allowing over a million Mormons to settle there since their first arrival in 1847.

2. **The Bays,** like the Chesapeake, Massachusetts, New York, Tampa, Galveston and San Francisco have assumed historical importance as maritime and commercial centers. They have served as fishing,

boating, beach sites and as well as for living nearby, and as ports of entry for waves of immigrants entering the U.S. by ship.

3. **Cliffs** and **bluffs** have been used by tribes of marauding bands of enemies risking their lives in order to scale steep walls commonly used as security measures by the dwellers within. The palisades in New Jersey was the scene of the infamous duel between Burr and Hamilton in 1804, with Hamilton dying from a gunshot wound – never to allow dueling again.

4. **Canals** have performed a vital economic function by neutralizing the land between barriers enabling cargoes to be transported over water routes. They also served as conduits for the supply of irrigation water. The 363 mile long Erie Canal, opened in 1825, was the frontrunner for subsequently built "Big Ditches" connecting rivers, lakes and man-made trench excavations. It linked New York City with Lake Erie and opened the gateway to the West.

5. **Canyons** Canyons are steep-walled valleys or gorges in a plateau mountainous area. Though their spectacular views are easy on the eyes, yet difficult afoot for transit. Situated throughout the West they have become prime tourist attractions, the most popular being the Grand Canyon of the Colorado River, listed as one of the Seven Natural Wonders of the World. It is 217 miles long and from 4-18 miles wide.

6. **Capes** A cape is a narrow piece of land jutting into the sea. During the age of exploration of America's Atlantic Coast the protruding capes were often the first sightings of land for sea captains eager to set forth a territorial claim. In 1620 the historic boat Mayflower anchored on Cape Cod, Massachusetts, leaving 103 Pilgrim separatists to disembark there founding Plymouth Colony, the first colonial settlement in the United States. Its maritime orientation has enriched the site for decades, with the site becoming a foremost center for the whaling industry. A vacation on the Cape has been considered to be a "must" vacation for many of today's Americans.

7. **Piedmonts** are fertile, rolling lands along the foot of mountain ranges. A major Piedmont lies between the Appalachian Mountains

and the Atlantic Coastal Plain. In the 1800's farmers were drawn to the Piedmont region and planted such crops as tobacco, vegetables and "King Cotton". That crop made slavery and plantation life profitable. Agricultural based Piedmonts are situated in Colorado and California where citrus and deciduous fruits thrive under ideal weather conditions. Also of importance was the discovery of gold there in 1848, bringing on the gold rush of hordes of people – eventually making California number one in U.S. population.

Place-names dealing with odd-sounding locales are likely to be full of intrigue. They may be a high-bar challenge for all who are curious about the "hows and whys" of their early formulations. Clues may aid in the solving of peculiar, if not fascinating, place-name origins. On the other hand, probable causes and inferences may peter out, leaving the investigator mystified and bewildered.

Many place-names started in the so-called "Wild West," which may offer a rationale for their components of humor and oddity. They tended, at times, not to be guided by absolute propriety and tradition. Their interrelationship aroused listeners to the mirth and fiction of joke-tellers and story.

The list of names that follow may seem very macabre, in some instances quite scary. Others reflect subtleties, puns and dual meanings with their entertaining wordings. The multi letters in the name CHAUBUNAGUNGAMAUG POND (MA), would require a very large envelope for addressing.

Abbreviations have been used for the states and are listed here:

Alaska	AK	Maine	ME	Oklahoma	OK
Alabama	AL	Maryland	MD	Oregon	OR
Arizona	AZ	Massachusetts	MA	Pennsylvania	PA
Arkansas	AR	Michigan	MI	Rhode Island	RI
California	CA	Minnesota	MN	South Carolina	SC
Colorado	CO	Mississippi	MS	South Dakota	SD
Connecticut	CT	Missouri	MO	Tennessee	TN
Delaware	DE	Montana	MT	Texas	TX
Florida	FL	Nebraska	NB	Utah	UT
Georgia	GA	Nevada	NV	Vermont	VT
Idaho	ID	New Hampshire	NH	Virginia	VA
Illinois	IL	New Jersey	NJ	Washington	WA
Indiana	IN	New Mexico	NM	West Virginia	WV
Iowa	IA	New York	NY	Wisconsin	WI
Kansas	KS	North Carolina	NC	Wyoming	WY
Kentucky	KY	North Dakota	ND		
Louisiana	LA	Ohio	OH		

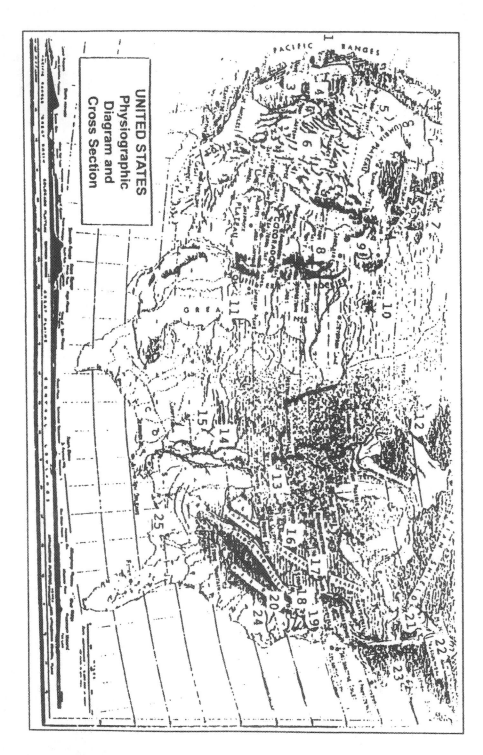

UNITED STATES
Physiographic
Diagram and
Cross Section

KEY TO LANDFORMS OF THE UNITED STATES

1. Coast Ranges
2. Cascade Range
3. Central Valley
4. Sierra Nevada
5. Columbia Plateau
6. Basin and Range Province
7. Rocky Mountains (Northern)
8. Rocky Mountains (Southern)
9. Wyoming Basin
10. Black Hills
11. Great Plains
12. Superior Uplands
13. Central Lowlands
14. Ozark Plateau
15. Ouachitas
16. Interior Low Plateau
17. Appalachian Plateau
18. Ridge and Valley Province
19. Great Smokies
20. Piedmont Upland
21. Adirondacks
22. New England Uplands and Mountains
23. Seaboard Lowlands
24. Atlantic Coastal Plain
25. Gulf Coastal Plain

GEOGRAPHICAL TERMS MENTIONED IN TEXT

BAY- 1. An inlet of the ocean or part of the ocean bordering on land and partly surrounded by land. 2. Any small body of water set off from the main body of an ocean, lake, or gulf.

BAYOU- A slow, sluggish stream; usually used to describe inlets from the Gulf of Mexico or from the Mississippi River.

BEACH- The pebbly or sandy shore of the sea or of a lake which is washed by the waves.

CANAL- A man-made channel filled with water used for navigation, irrigation, or drainage.

CANYON- A deep, narrow valley having high, steep slopes; example, the Grand Canyon.

CAPE- A narrow piece of land projecting into the sea.

CAVE- A deep, hollowed-out area under the earth's surface.

CHANNEL- 1. A narrow strip of water. 2. The part of a stream or body of water which affords the best passage for vessels; usually because of its greater depth.

CLIFF- The steep, rocky face of a bluff.

COAST- Land along the sea.

COUNTRY- 1. A nation or area of land which is politically controlled by one government. 2. Thinly populated areas as compared with a city.

CREEK- A natural stream of running water larger than a brook and smaller than a river.

DALE- A small valley.

DELTA- Earth that is dropped by running water when a stream flows into the still water of a lake or ocean.

DESERT- A large area of land with little or no moisture or vegetation.

GLEN- A small valley usually long, narrow, and steep sided.

GORGE- A narrow passage between steep mountains or hills; a steep, rocky ravine.

GULF- An area of water bordering on, and lying within a curved coastline; usually larger than a bay and smaller than a sea; sometimes nearly surrounded by land.

HARBOR- A sheltered body of water where ships anchor and are protected from storms.

HILL- A small area of land that is higher than the land around it.

ISLAND- An area of land surrounded by water.

LAKE- An inland body of water usually of considerable size.

MEADOW- An area of level land where grass is grown and usually cut for hay.

MESA- A flat topped, rocky hill with steeply sloping sides.

MINE- A pit from which coal, minerals, or precious stones are taken by digging.

MOUNTAIN- A lofty elevation on the earth's surface.

MOUNTAIN RANGE- A series of connecting mountains.

PENNINSULA- A piece of land nearly surrounded by water and attached to a larger area of land or the mainland by an isthmus.

PIEDMONT- An area of rolling land along the foot of a mountain range.

PLAIN- A nearly level area of land usually of considerable size.

PLATEAU- A large, level, or nearly level area of elevated land.

RAPIDS- Part of a stream where the water flows very swiftly over rocks.

RIVER- A large stream of water of natural origin, which drains an area of land and flows into another river or body of water.

SEA- 1. A large body of water partly or nearly surrounded by land. 2. Sometimes used to describe all the ocean area of the world as a unit.

SOUND- A long and rather narrow body of water, larger than a strait, connecting two large bodies of water or separating a large island from the mainland.

STREAM- A flow of moving water usually of natural origin.

SUMMIT- Highest part of a hill or mountain.

TOWN- 1. A large village. 2. In some states the same as a township.

TRIBUTARY- A stream which flows into another stream; usually used to describe the one which considerably increases the size of the stream into which it flows.

VALLEY- The land between hills or mountains, usually containing a stream.

WOODS- An area of land covered with trees; a forest.

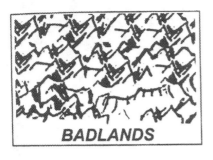

BADLANDS

BASINS

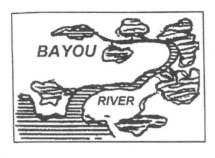

BAYOUS

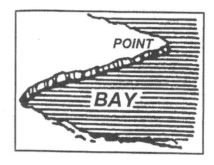

BAYS

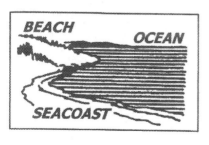

BEACHES

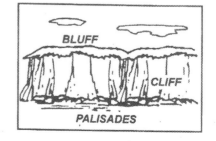

BLUFFS/CLIFFS/PALISADES

BUTTES

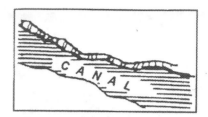

CANALS

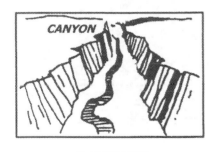

CANYONS

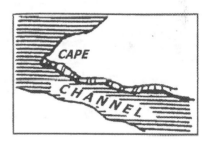

CAPES

COASTAL PLAINS

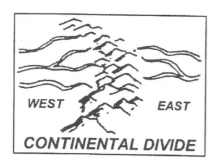

CONTINENTAL DIVIDE

CONTINENTAL SHELVES

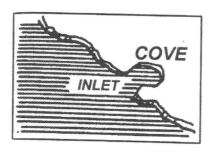

COVES

DELTAS

DESERTS

FALL LINES

GREAT PLAINS

GULFS

HARBORS

HILLS

ISLANDS

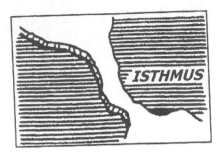

ISTHMUSES

KEYS

LAKES

MESAS

MOUNTAINS

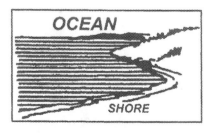

OCEANS

PASSES AND GAPS

PENINSULAS

PIEDMONTS

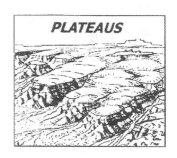

PLATEAUS

RELIEF (ELEVATION), PEAK

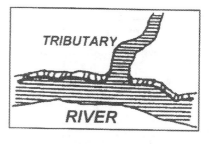

RIVERS

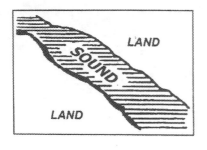

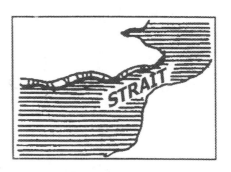

STRAITS/SOUNDS

SPRINGS

SWAMPS/MARSHES

VALLEYS

WATERFALLS

III.

~

NATIVE AMERICAN (INDIAN) NAMES

The Europeans, arriving in what is presently considered the United States after the 1500's, encountered a diverse group of Native Americans, historically known as Indians. Their tribes numbered in the hundreds, each group having rather distinct life-styles depending on the regions of their habitation.

Those Indians living along the northwest seacoasts combined agricultural pursuits with fishing and seeking shellfish beds. Indians populating interior basins and plains hunted large-size buffaloes and deer. The climate and regional resources determined the kinds of berries, crops and animals found in their own distinctive settings. Each of the lands and water bodies assumed place-names which aided Indians in locating and claiming special places, often at the exclusion of others.

Communications and trading with nearby tribesmen and white itinerants relied on primitive signs and barter. The broad array of tribal groups spoke over a thousand different languages. Many tribes assigned different names to a similar site. They usually related to the surroundings they were most familiar with. Battles fought, discoveries and experiences with sometimes unwelcome intruders, and those whom would transgress their domains, were remembered in their place-namings. Today, in some manner and word usage, they are still printed on physical and political maps of the United States. Some of the Indian references have merged with European languages, affording map users orientations and understandings of history and geography.

During the early years of European settlement in the United States, and in the decades that followed, a number of major Indian tribes were disbursed throughout the land. Each large clan practiced their own brand of beliefs of good and evil. Most often they were influenced by a chief or leader called a shaman. The various regional tribes claimed hundreds of individual groupings having their own local mini-civilizations or cultures. Their unique life-styles led to vocabularies and terminologies that proved to be, in part, the forerunners of present-day name usage that tend to inundate American maps.

As settlers, buffalo hunters, prospectors and others moved into the western United States they were confronted by scores of Indian tribes, many of which were hostile to them. In the 1870's in order to alleviate the situation and the rising number of clashes, the federal government's officials, with little understanding of the Native American's plight, decided to place many tribes on reservations throughout the land. Yet the majority were confined to sites in the newly acknowledged states and territories. By 1890 the reservations were "home" to countless numbers of Native Americans, mainly including large groupings of Algonquians, Creeks, Chickasaws, Comanche, Chewkees, Apaches, Pueblos and Sioux. Additional major tribes were classified as Zunis, Apaches, Hopis, Navajos, Shoshones, Blackfeet, Iroquois and Nez Perces.

Later each of the major groups had enclaves of lesser clans, some of whom moved on to reservations in distant locations where they were treated more humanly and were able to get schooling and learn specific skills, like fabric weaving and jewelry making. Some of those tribes included Seminoles, Catawsas, Tuscaroras, Tritelos, Powhatans, Delawares, Susquehannas, Iroquois and Mohigans. Though scattered about, their names remain with us, both present and past. More than likely every state's heritage possesses some reference to its Indian tribal origins.

Locations of American Indian Tribes
At the Time of European Settlement

Detailed maps of the United States can tell us much about the extent and location of Native Americans. They also provide insights on how many lived within physical environments. Their tribal names can be found on lakes, rivers, creeks, falls, national monuments, mountains, reservation and cities.

Indicative of these tribal names one can easily find the names and origins of a few dissimilar clans printed on maps. There are Pueblos, Mohawks, Delawares, Utes, Yakimas and Winnebagos. Also Pawnees, Comanchees, Sioux, Crows, Tuscaroras, Cheyennes, Susquehannas, Mojaves, Shawnees and Dakotas can add to the list.

Some of the smaller units combined a word with an Indian meaning with the language of the Anglo-Saxons. A case in point refers to AMBO, an Algonquin term, probably meaning something hollowed out, thus a valley-like depression. In time this was blended with the name of the fourth earl of PERTH (1648-1716), becoming PERTH AMBOY, N.J., an important seaport of that time.

It is generally agreed that Native American were fundamentally Mongoloid. Indigenous to northeast Asia, they crossed the 45 mile Bering Strait into present-day Alaska eons of years ago. They apparently migrated southward, many settling in parts of contemporary United States. They were primarily fishermen, hunters and food gathers. Much of their subsistence was dictated by climates and regional fauna and flora. Uniformity of language was uncommon. There was a wide distribution of "native tongues" so to speak. The linguistic situation amongst the Native American illustrated a great number of distinct languages. Each flourished within their own confined areas. For example there were groups of Sioux and Shoshone languages, each having unique etymologies. A list of selected Native American (Indian) place-names state origins and their synoptic meanings follow:

Alabama   Indian for tribal town.

Arizona   Spanish version of Pima Indian word for "little spring place", or AZTEC ARIZUMA, meaning "silver bearing."

Arkansas   French variant of QUAPAW (downstream people), a Siouan people. river place."

Delaware   Named for Lord De La Warr, early governor of Virginia; first applied to river, then to Indian tribe (Lenni-Lenape), and the state.

Idaho   A coined name with an invented Indian meaning: "gem of the mountains."

Illinois   French for ILLINI or "land of ILLINI", Algonquin word meaning men or warriors.

Indiana   Means "land of the Indians."

Iowa   Indian word variously translated as "one who puts to sleep" or "beautiful land."

Kansas   Sioux word for "south wind people."

Kentucky   Indian word variously translated as "dark and bloody ground," "meadowland" and "land of tomorrow."

Massachusetts   From Indian tribe named after "large hill place."

Michigan   From Chippewa words, MICI GAM meaning "great water," after the lake of the same name.

Minnesota   From Dakota Sioux word meaning "cloudy water," or "sky-tinted water of the Minnesota River."

Missouri   An Algonquin Indian term meaning "river of the big canoes."

Nebraska   From Omaha or Otos Indian word meaning "broad water" or "flat river," describing the Platte River.

Ohio   Iroquois word for "fine" or "good river."

Tennessee   TANASI was the name of a Cherokee village on the Little Tennessee River.

Utah   From a Navajo word meaning "upper" or "higher up" as applied to a Shoshone tribe called UTE. The Spanish form is YUTTA.

Wisconsin   An Indian name, spelled OUISCONSIN and MESCONSING by early chronicles. Believed to mean "grassy place" in Chippewa.

Wyoming   From the Algonquin words for "large prairie place" or "at the big place" or "great plains."

TRIBAL NAMES and INDIAN TRAILS
(Delaware Indians – Lenni Lenape)

■ **TRIBAL NAMES**

1 MINISINK
2 POMPTON
3 TAPPAN
4 ACQUACKANONK
5 HACKENSACK
6 ROXITICUS
7 RARITAN
8 NESHANICS
9 TOPONOMESE
10 NAVESINK
11 MATAWANS
12 ASSUNPINK
13 SANHICAIS
14 CALCEFAR
15 RANCOCAS
16 ATSIONS
17 METEDECONK
18 YACOMANSHAGHKING
19 ARMEWAMEX
20 ERIWONEX
21 MANTAS
22 ASAMOHACKING
23 SICONESE
24 NARATICONGS
25 KAHANSUK
26 SEWAPOIS
27 KECHEMECHES
28 TIRANS

■ **MAJOR GROUPS**

MUNSEE (MINSI)
UNAMI
UNALACHTIGO

MUNEE

UNAMI

UNALACHTIGO

Minisink Trail
Alhamatunk Trail
Trail
Old Cape Road
Manahawkin
Trail
Burlington Trail
Cohansey Tr.

MEANING of NAMES

MINSI – "People of the stony ground"
UNAMI – "People down the river"
UNALACHTIGO –
    "People near the ocean"

Accurate names once conferred for a place may have been lost in the lapse of millions of moments in time. They may deliberately have been misplaced or overlooked by earlier town "fathers" for selfish purposes. City Council members may have been jealous or spiteful in assigning names for places, especially those that reflected names bearing possessive claims in their nomenclature. Geographic inclusions may have been nondescript or less recognizable. Later investigations may have uncovered misinformation in fact-finding about a place, therefore justifying the discard of the source of the name origin.

In 1840 a site in Illinois was given the name Nauvoo by Joseph Smith, the Mormon Church leader. When he left the town the name was abandoned.

In the United States, despite the naming of places since the "birth of a nation", an attempt at good old American jesting may have over reached into a bewildering labeling of two small villages in Texas and North Dakota. They were once actually called NAMELESS. Once, years ago, while tourists were viewing the depths of NAMELESS CAVE in South Dakota, the guide afforded them a chance to name the cavern being studied. A year later NAMELESS received the most votes.

Sometimes a new member of a family is given a name based on lengthy deliberations. Similarly, as the story goes, at an Iroquois pow wow in upstate New York, no agreement could be reached for the naming of a nearby dominant hill. Consequently, the Chief of the tribe took it upon himself to bestow a name. Fittingly he selected NONAMES HILL.

Educational curriculum planners and school publishers have found a kind of renaissance in their humanities course offerings. Today, more than ever, college bound students study mythical and classical literature, often correlated with social studies. Place-names appear in both disciplines. The courses tell stories about gods, heroes and imagined places pertaining to ancient Greek and Roman times. The accounts are in a distinct-literary style.

Research has found a small amount of United States place-names associated with this type of cultural learning.

Athena (NY), Attica (NY), Clio (SC), Ithaca (NY), Jupiter (FL), Mars (SC), Pandora (WA), Palmyra (PA), Rome (NY), Romulus (MI), Styx (TX), Syracuse (NY), Troy (NY), Venus (NB), Xenia (OH).

Representative Native American (Indian) Name Origins (Abridged in part from a dictionary of Place-names, George R. Stewart)

Delaware (DE) A cape in the area called for the governor, La Warr, later written as Delaware. Later an Indian tribe of that area.

Mohegan (CT) From a village inhabited by an Algonquian tribe.

Miami (FL) A Muskogean term applied to the "very large" river.

Iroquois (MI) Indian tribal named before 1800, due to invading Iroquois.

Osage (OK) A tribal name in French (1673) context as Ouchage.

Oswego (NY) Iroquoian "flowing out," meaning mouth of the river.

Waukegan (IL) Algonquian for "house, fort or trading-post". Named in 1849.

Yuma (AZ) It is from a local Indian tribe.

Wantagh (NY) Named after an early local Indian chief WYANDANCE.

Comanche (MT) From an Indian horse, sole survivor of the battle of Big Horn, 1876.

Shoshone (CO) Name of the variant Indian tribal name of a mountain peak in CO.

Niagara (NY) An Iroquoian name "neck of land" – not river or fall.

Allegheny (PA) An English adoption of the Algonquian "most beautiful".

Hackensack (NJ) From the name of an Indian village and tribe.

Hialeah (FL) Probably Seminole "beautiful prairie".

Hokah (MN) Sioux "root" or "crane" or the name of a Siouan chief.

Kalamazoo (MI) Algonquian for "it smokes, troubled with smoke".

Hoboken (NJ) Possibly of Dutch origin but maybe an Algonquian term, tobacco pipe.

Lapwai (ID) From the Nez Perce Indians, probably "butter-fly stream".

Mackinaw (MI) It is Algonquian meaning "big turtle at".

Quinnipiac (CT) Algonquian for "turning point" to mark a change in a direction of travel.

Suwannee (GA) Of Indian origin, possibly Muskogean, after a town on its river bank.

Tamarack (FL) An Algonquian word for a tree found near water, lakes and swamps.

Tonopah (NV) Shoshone for "greasewood-spring".

Locktsapopa River (FL) Seminole "an eating place".

Mossback Meadow (UT) Algonquian meaning "much water, overflowed".

Monongalia County (WV) From the Monongalia River – an Indian name Latinized.

Oskkosh (WI) For a well-known Menominee chief (1795 – 1858)

Paducak (KY) It is from a local (CHICKASAW) chief.

Pequonock (CT) Algonquian: "small farm field".

Sagamore (ME) An Algonquian word for "chief".

Ute (UT) From an Indian tribe to Utah in 1850 upon becoming a territory.

American explorers and settlers encountered distinct populations within the Native American groupings. It is estimated that 70% of the tribal units spoke eight different languages. Specific tribes tended to occupy a region each manifesting a rather similar manner of selecting names and meanings based on their immediate surroundings. Discrete tribal names and their locations can be found by referring to the American Indian Tribes map enclosed in this volume.

A composite listing of selective Native American tribal information follows. They comprise names, locations and place-name origins. Algonquian, Sioux, Cherokee, Muskogean, Iroquois, Shawnee and Creek names are included:

Kenosha (WI) "pike, pickerel", Kennebec (ME) "long neck", Schenectady (NY) "beyond pines", Roanoke (VA) "white shell place", Yacolt (WA) "haunted place", Chattanooga (TN) "rock rising to a point", Mankato (MN) earth blue (green), Ottumwa (IA) "swift water", Tallahassee (FL) "town old", Erie (PA) "the cat nation", Michigan (MI) "big lake", Manahawkin (NJ) "island small", Okeechobee (FL) "water big", Menominee (WI) "wild rice".

Olathe (KS) "fine, beautiful", Okobojo (SD) "planting in spaces", Raritan (NJ) "stream overflow", Connecticut "long tidal river," Cullasaja (NC) "honey-locust place," Miami (FL) "very large," Tuscaloosa (AL) "warrior-black," Secaucus (NJ) salt-sedge/wet ground marsh and Sioux City (IA) from the populous tribes that roamed the Great Plains and Central Lowlands.

IV.

~

FOREIGN LANGUAGE DERIVATION NAMES

The number of foreign language place-names emerging from French and Spanish sources are considerable. They stem from all aspects of history, locations, religions, literature and the past rulers of each country's motherland. Their distinctive collection of place-names representing many Europe's renown figures, as well as national cultures and traditions are remembered, duly honored by their appearances on American-made maps. Many have been identified and incorporated into the English lingo and delineated on drawings and printing of some portion of the earth's topography.

Shortly after the British became entrenched in the new world, especially along the eastern seaboard, the Spanish people extended their vast territorial claims by implanting their language in many seemingly boundless parts of North America. Forerunning words, like San or La precede many Hispanic place-names.

The Dutch started a colony in 1609 called New Amsterdam, renamed New Netherlands, eventually becoming New York. The Swedes and Finns also became settlers along the Delaware River offering the place-names of Finn's Point and Swedsboro, both cities in New Jersey.

NEW MORSHOLM 1647
UPLANDT 1643 · FT BEVERSREDE 1643
· 1643
· FT. NASSAU 1623
FT. NEW GOTTENBURG 1643

FT CHRISTINA
(WILMINGTON)
1638

FT CASIMIR
(NEW CASTLE)
1651
VARCKENSKILL 1641
(NEW ENGLAND 1635)
FT TRINITY
1654
NEW AMSTEL
1656
FT NEW
ELFSBORG
1643

DELAWARE
BAY

SOUTH BORDER CLAIMED
BY SWEDEN 1642

NEW SWEDEN
1638-1655;
NEW NETHERLAND
1655-1664

· ZWAANENDAEL 1631

Names of Swedish settlements are underscored

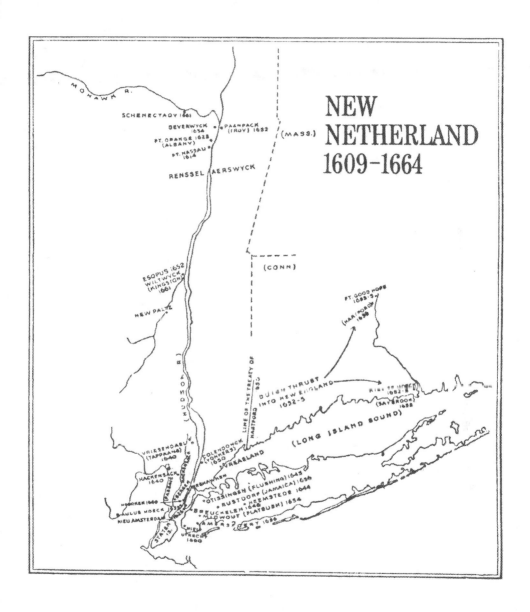

English Colonies, Charter Grants, 1660-1700, and Frontier of Settlement, 1700

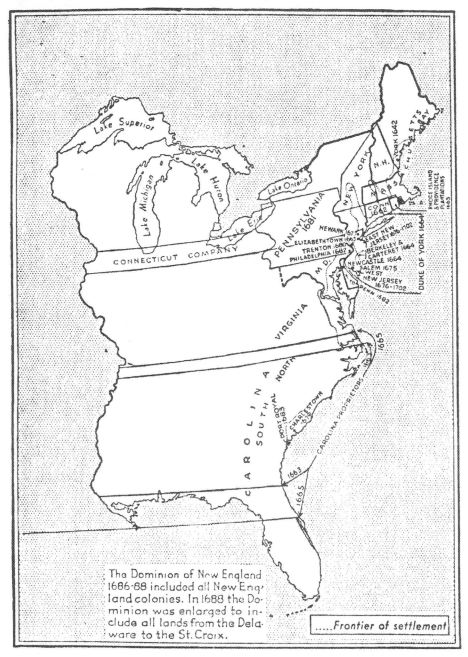

The Dominion of New England 1686-88 included all New England colonies. In 1688 the Dominion was enlarged to include all lands from the Delaware to the St. Croix.

.....Frontier of settlement

PLACE-NAME ORIGINS: ENGLISH, DUTCH, GEOGRAPHIC, RELIGIOUS

The twenty-one counties of New Jersey.

ESTIMATE: ONE THIRD OF THE REVOLUTIONARY WAR TOOK PLACE IN NEW JERSEY

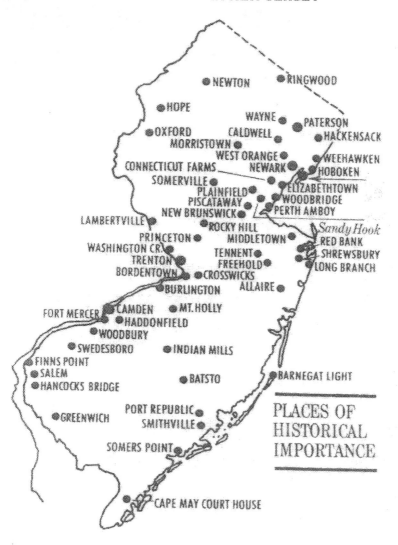

NOTE: WASHINGTON CR -
Site of Washington's crossing the Delaware River
12/25/1776

Later tens of thousands of Scotch-Irish, German and other European immigrants started communities with each mother tongue's tribute to the naming of a place.

Implants of French place-names abound throughout the land, found wherever the French speaking explorers and fur trappers set foot.

It should be noted that numerous United States place-names and geographic features found in various regions of the country bear alterations in their names. They may reflect a foreign usage of a syllable at the beginning or ending of a word. Prefixes are inserted at the start and suffixes go to make up the endings of foreign words.

The Spanish language names are chiefly located in the southwest region of the United States and French names are found throughout Louisiana and along the Mississippi River. Volunteers with foreign backgrounds have contributed to America's success in the Revolutionary War. Outstanding among them were the Marquis de Lafayette, Johann de Kalb, Casmir Pulaski, and Baron von Steuben, all being graced by having American places named for them. Appreciation for Sebastian Cabot, an English explorer and Giovanni Verrazano, an Italian seaman in the 16th century, have a special place and a bridge named for them. Another Italian explorer Amerigo Vespucci, is said to have discovered "America".

LESSER KNOWN SELECT FOREIGN SOURCES OF U.S. PLACE-NAME, MEANINGS

Country	Name of Place	Lat/Long Coordinates	Origin; Named For; Meaning
F	Dubuque, IA	42.30N/90.43W	First settler in 1785
F	Marquette, MI	46.32N/87.25W	17th century missionary, explorer
F	Cape Girardeau, MO	31.17N/89.32W	Trader, Sieur Jean B. Girardot, 1704
F	La Crosse, WI	43.18N/91.14W	Stick used in Indian game
F	Prairie du Chien, WI	43.02N/91.28W	Prairie of the Dog
F	Napoleon, OH	41.20N/84.10W	Napoleon Bonaparte
F	Sault Sainte Marie, MI	46.29N/84.21W	"falls of St. Mary"
F	Fond du Lac, WI	43.47N/88.29W	"end of lake"
F	Eau Claire, WI	44.47N/91.32W	clear water
F	Belleville, NJ	40.44N/74.10W	pretty view
G	Rhineland, WI	43.39N/89.25W	river flowing through Germany
G	Germantown, OH	39.35N/84.25W	settlement of Germans in 1683
G	Potsdam, NY	44.40N/75.00W	for German city
D	Rensselaer, OH	41.00N/87.10W	for Kiliaen van Rensselaer
D	Holland, MI	42.45N/86.10W	settlers from European country
D	Amsterdam, NY	42.56N/74.11W	for the city in Holland
D	Van Wert, OH	40.50N/84.35W	famous militiaman of Dutch lineage
R	Russian River, CA	38.59N/123.10W	early settlement of Russians
R	Lake Odessa, TX	42.50N/85.15W	for the Black Seaport
S	Santa Cruz, Mts., CA	37.30N/122.19W	discovered on Holy Cross Day
S	Laredo, TX	27.31N/99.29W	after town in Spain, founded in 1755
S	El Dorado, KS	37.49N/96.51W	golden or gilden land
SW	Stockholm, ME	47.05N/68.08W	from the city in Sweden

F=French, G=German, D=Dutch, R=Russian, S=Spanish, SW=Swedish

Selected Geographic Foreign Terms Found With U.S. Place-names

(shed) bath or spa, (banco) bank, (berg) hill, (burg) town, (cap) cape, (canon) canyon, (casa) house, (cima) summit, (costa) coast, (desierto) desert, (detroit) strait, (dorf) village, (estado) east, (feld) field, (foret) forest, (feuente) spring, (fort) ford, (golfe) gulf, (ile) island, (isla) island, (lago) lake, (llanos) plains, (mar) sea, (mesa) tableland, (mina) mine, (mont) mountain, (mund) mouth, (nez) point, (norte) north, (occidental) west, (oriental) east, (paso) pass, (pico) peak, (playa) beach, (pont) bridge, (prado) meadow, (pueblo) town, (rio) river, (senu) bay, (sierra) range, (sud) south, (terra) earth, (valle) valley, (villa) town.

The act of transferring place-names from one place to another has long been an acceptable, if not desirable, practice throughout the United States' history. The frequency of renamings came about due to a person's nostalgia for "ye ole sod", or for the remembrance of a past incident that may have taken place there, or for sheer pride. There may have been an occurrence that prompted the birth of a name for posterity.

Names that tend to be compatible with original names are respectfully preceded with the adjective "new", as in New London, New Rochelle, New Brunswick or New York.

The proliferation of new immigrants into the metropolitan areas of the U.S. has accelerated the growth of foreign theme restaurants and their accompanying culinary menus. They tend to reflect the names of foods and languages of such countries as Italy, Spain, France, China, India, Korea and assorted oriental cultures. Their places of business can be identified by foreign name signs situated over welcoming entrances.

PARTIAL TRANSLATIONS, GEOGRAPHIC MEANINGS AND EXAMPLES OF FOREIGN TERMS

Fr=French, Sp=Spanish, Ger=German, Du=Dutch

Term	Country	Meaning	Example
Alp	Ger	mountain	Alpine (TX)
Alto	Sp	height	Alto (LA)
Arroyo	Sp	brook, stream	Arroyo Grande (CA)
Back	Ger	brook	Bathtub Spring (NY)
Bad	Ger	bath, spa	Carlsbad (CA), Bathtub Spring (WY)
Bahia	Sp	bay, gulf	Bahia Honda (FL)
Baja	Sp	"descent"	La Bajada (NM)
Bayou	Fr	river outlet	Bastrop Bayou (TX)
Boca	Sp	mouth	Boca Raton (FL)
Bois	Fr	forest, wood	Bois Blanc (MI)
Bolson	Sp	flat-floor, desert valley	Bolsa (CA)
Burg	Ger	town	Hattiesburg (MS)
Burgh	Ger	town	Plattsburgh (NY)
Cabezo	Sp	summit	Cabezon Peak (NM)
Campo	Sp	field, plain	El Campo (TX)
Canon	Sp	canyon	Canon City (CO)
Cap	Fr	cape	Cap au Gris (MO)
Casa	Sp	house	Casa Grande (AZ)
Champ	Fr	field	Champaign (IL)
Cordillera	Sp	mountain chain	Cordillera (CA)
Costa	Sp	coast	Costa Mesa (CA)
Detroit	Fr	strait	Detroit (MI)
Dorp	Du	village	New Dorp (NY)
Eau	Fr	water	Eau Clare (WI)

Term	Country	Meaning	Example
Field	Ger	plain, field	Fairfield (CT)
Ile	Fr	island	Isle au Bois (MO)
Lac	Fr	lake	Fond du Lac (WI)
Lago	Sp	lake	Lago (ID)
Loma	Sp	long, low hill	Point Loma (CA)
Mar	Sp	sea	Mar Vista (CA)
Mesa	Sp	flat, table topped mountain	Mesa (AZ)
Mont	Fr	mountain	Montpelier (VT)
Monte	Sp	mountain	Monte Vista (CA)
Nord	Ger	north	Nord (CA)
Occidental	Sp	western	Occidental (CA)
Pico	Sp	mountain peak	Pico (CA)
Playa	Sp	shore, beach	Playas (NM)
Pueblo	Sp	town, village	Pueblo (CA)
Puerto	Sp	port, harbor	Puerto de Luna (NM)
Punta	Sp	point	Punta Gorda (FL)
Ria	Sp	estuary	Rialto (CA)
Rio	Sp	river	Rio Grande (TX)
Riviere	Fr	river	Riviera Beach (FL)
Sable	Fr	sand	Sable (FL)
Salto	Sp	waterfall	Salton Sea (CA)
Sierra	Sp	mountain range	Sierra Blanca (TX)
Stadt	Ger	city, town	Carlstadt (NJ)
Terra	Sp	earth, land	Tierra Haute (IN)
Valle	Sp	valley	Valle Vista (CA)
Villa	Sp	town	Villa Park (CA)
Ville	Fr	town, city	Fayetteville (NC)
Wald	Ger	forest, woodland	Waldorf (MD)

V.

~

COMMEMORATIVE AND COMMENDATORY NAMES

The honoring of persons and incidents marking of a nation's past, have been translated onto English names and terminology, eventually becoming visible on maps, both physical and cultural.

Pride and nostalgia have entered into the selections of place-names remembrances. They frequently may connote the heroic attributions of individuals, their deeds and/or their anniversaries. The names may refer to distant places and past events.

Remarkable cartographic features adorn many maps. Prideful commendations of a subtle type have joined in a dictionary of map words appropriately adapted for inclusion in an array of map graphics. A good number of commemorative names have been coined by the recalls. Though hazy, the sensations and emotions experienced by settlers and pioneers have been translated onto map representations. Their place-name applications have become perpetual on maps due to a long term usage of their special place in the toponomy classifications. Commendatory biblical names of places are found to be plentiful throughout the United States. They conjure respect for preferred religious affiliations and church teachings.

Commemorative names are given to honor particular persons or places. The commemoration is usually meant to memorialize people with a fitting tribute, at times appearing on statues, monuments or by naming a place after them.

Commendatory statements are designed to commend or praise. Laudatory, positive descriptive words about beneficial or beautiful things are deemed to be commendatory recognitions.

Celebrations about commemorative days have contributed much to our American life, culture and heritage. The idea of having an anniversary celebration or birthday party took roots in Europe hundreds of years ago. Then, people had the notion that good and evil spirits lurking nearby became noticeably present on that day, causing harm to the celebrants. They were bent on preventing that from happening.

As a means of detracting from the fear and threat, friends and relatives of the birthday person would gather around the celebrant on the day of the year that marked their birth, eat with him or her, and bestow the person with presents and good wishes. This was done, in a commemorative way, to overcome any negative casts. These wholesome blessings, it was believed, would then bring out the good spirits.

Today, the custom of honoring, paying respect for the honoree continues by demonstrating affection and admiration for the individual, or episode being recognized. Therefore, holidays and celebrations are interchangeable. Holidays (originally a "holy day") were celebrated thousands of years ago when people held religious festivals to honor their gods. Then feasts and rites were held to acknowledge their dead, or pay homage to them. It was also customary to offer thankful prayers at successful harvest times. Some of those practices of the holidays often continue on, being handed down from generation to generation.

In the United States special celebrations are most often categorized according to their purpose. They are religious holidays (Christmas), patriotic holidays (Washington's Birthday), legal holidays (Veteran's

Day) and (Election Day), special holidays (Arbor Days), traditional days (Mother's Day), as well as many other reasons to take time to follow a custom to pause and reflect on the true meaning of the day, set aside for national introspection and to commemorate and launch commendations to the deserving. The customs and cultures of diverse peoples to honor some highly cherished ideal, a contribution of a great person, or some memorable episodes in history, as practiced in the United States is something to be admired. As well as the appreciation for the day's theme, patriotism or love of country is enhanced.

The theme of the special day is often recognized by a place-name on a map, or with an official remembrance, leaving an everlasting commitment of honor.

The Mall in Washington, D.C., by example, is a site that provides two types of commemorative attractions; the Vietnam Memorial, list the names of thousands of servicemen and servicewomen making the supreme sacrifice during that conflict. A second, at another site, is the stature of Abraham Lincoln, a startling likeness to one of the nation's greatest presidents. Both are man-made. Also on the Mall there is a large statue of Martin Luther King, the famous civil rights leader.

For examples of commendatory places where viewers are held in sublime awe, the Grand Canyon and the fall foliage of the New England states meet the criteria of natural beauty. Both are places that reveal the utmost in grandeur. So too are Bryce Canyon in Utah and Yosemite National Park in California. Also, in keeping with the underlying intent of identifying commendatory places, Palm Beach, California, Niagara Falls, New York and the Blue Ridge Mountains of Virginia could readily be added to the list.

It should be noted that in the past decade laws that go to rebuild older American cities and their environs are now in effect. The "green" revolution, with its objective to make urban areas more environmentally correct, has won plaudits from city planners throughout the country. In many places a balance between modernity and older city assets has developed. Construction of high rise buildings has been booming. New roads are alleviating traffic congestion and are now more user friendly.

Famous America vocalists have extolled the virtues of New York, Chicago and San Francisco in song. In the renditions of the very popular melody, Route 66, the words take the listener on a trip over Kingman (Arizona), Barstow (California) and San Bernardino in the same state.

There are countless numbers of lesser-known persons and events that have had their names applied to geographic sites throughout the United States. Their designations are marked by heroic records, personified by positive characteristics and values. A random sampling follows:

John Muir (CA) nature lover and writer, Thomas Edison (NJ) inventor, Daniel Webster (MO) orator and statesman, Paul Revere (MA) patriot, warned of British soldiers, Kit Carson (NV) famous frontiersman, Pontiac (MI) great chief of the Ottawas, Robert Fulton (MO) inventor of the steamboat, Veteran (WY) in honor of servicemen, VN de Balboa (CA) discoverer of Pacific Ocean, George Darvey (OK) war hero admiral, Lewis and Clark (OR) in honor of their expedition, Com. Oliver Perry (NY) victor at Lake Erie battle.

A collection of Major American Cities and Their Name Origins

Albuquerque (NM) In honor of the Duke of Albuquerque, the Viceroy of New Spain.

Arlington (TX) Named after the Virginia estate of Robert E. Lee.

Atlanta (GA) In 1845 the Georgia Railroad took the name for its terminus in that state.

Austin (TX) For Stephen E. Austin, who brought the first Anglo settlers to Texas in the 1820's.

Baltimore (MD) Named after the founder of the colony of Maryland, Lord Baltimore.

Boston (MA) Named for the English port from which many Puritan to America came.

Charlotte (NC) In 1762 it was named Charlotte, after the new bride of King George III.

Cleveland (OH) Founded in 1796 and named after Moses Cleveland, a surveyor.

Columbus (OH) In honor of the famous explorer of the New World.

Dallas (TX) Named in 1846 after Vice President, George Mifflin Dallas.

Detroit (MI) Situated on the Detroit River between Lake Erie and Lake Huron (French: of the strait).

Fort Worth (TX) Named in 1849 after Gen. William J. Worth, commander of the U.S. Army in Texas.

Honolulu (HI) Means "sheltered harbor".

Houston (TX) Named after Sam Houston, the first president of the Republic of Texas.

Jacksonville (FL) Named for Maj. Gen. Andrew Jackson who led the U.S. campaign to take Florida from the Spanish.

Kansas City (MO) Situated on the confluence of the Kansas and Missouri rivers, named in 1889.

Long Beach (CA) Named after its 8.5 miles of Pacific beachfront.

Louisville (KY) Named after a French king.

Memphis (TN) After the ancient Egyptian city on the Nile.

Mesa (AZ) "table top," flat-topped raised area.

Miami (FL) "Big water" – a Seminole derivation.

Milwaukee (WI) "Beautiful land." Indian origin. millokee.

Minneapolis (MN) Hybrid of the Indian word minne meaning "water," and the Greek word for "city."

Nashville (TN) After Gen. Francis Nash of the Revolutionary Army.

New York (NY) Renamed from the Dutch for the Duke of York in 1673.

Omaha (NE) The name means "above all others on the stream."

Phoenix (AZ) The site is named after the mythical bird that rose from its own ashes.

Portland (OR) Named after the hometown in Maine of Francis Pettygrove, who won its name on a coin toss.

Sacramento (CA) Implying a place having a sacred significance.

San Antonio (TX) A mission known as the Alamo and Presidio in 1718.

San Francisco (CA) Named for Saint Francis by Spanish missionaries.

Seattle (WA) A name derived from the loose approximation of the name of the Squamish Chief Sealth.

Tucson (AZ) Means "village of the dark spring at the foot of the mountains."

Tulsa (OK) Under the Indian Removal Act of 1830 the tribe chose for their new home Tulsey, a corruption of Tallahassee.

VI.

~

NATIONAL AND ETHNOGRAPHIC (CULTURE) NAMES

E thnography is the study of specific cultures of groups, emphasizing their emotional attitudes, characteristics, languages, beliefs and folkways. The focus is often centered on the deep-seated heritages of political or occupational traits found within a nation or foreign land over a period of time.

The behavior patterns of a particular people may often lead to generalizations about their genesis and the many factors of a geographic disposition, especially name identifications of places where they have lived, or are presently living. The backgrounds and development of a national or religious people have affected the language of maps with their colorful name origins, a perpetuity well cherished and identified on map layouts. This unique kind of map may bolster the knowledge of lesser known civilizations.

Countries tend to have common histories and cultures based on the retelling of shared stories and accounts of people living at that time and events lacking authenticity, over a period of time, myths and fables have been uncovered. The exaggerations and distortions surrounding invalid circumstances may have been interpreted to be truthful and accounts were unintentionally passed about from person to person. They may have been couched with deceit in their word transmissions. This was the origin of certain place-names, which eventually emerged as certainties in geography books and on maps.

Places, in their early discoveries, were sometimes named in an impromptu moment. Undeserving political leaders were elevated to high pedestals despite questions about their integrity or contribution to the United States' record. Historians have reviewed many disparities and have challenged the accuracy of the Betsy Ross flag making narrative in Philadelphia, Pennsylvania. The validity of Washington (he never told a lie) tossing a silver dollar across the Potomac River was most certainly fictitious.

The biggest misconception some people have is the quasi-chauvinistic belief that Columbus "discovered" America.

The United States has developed a distinct set of values to live by. It is a culture based on a set of goals or principals that attempt to guide positive behavior by its citizens. Each state has embraced a motto of its own that underscores an inherent philosophy of righteousness. A composite of the words and expressions included in the mottoes give a valid inkling into American ideals, values and character. Representations follow herewith:

Liberty, independence, rule of the people, right of self-defense are stressed. Also mentioned in the terminology are hope, providence, peace, unity, equality, virtue, ambition, patriotism and trust in God are featured. A variety of U.S. places have adopted some of these fitting adjectives and nouns in their initial naming processes. All demonstrate a proud heritage.

A plethora of place-name origins are referenced throughout this book. Many deal with the essential qualities of American values. Most also show a propensity for exemplary virtues achieved since the founding of the country. Appropriate descriptive terminology and state connections preface the smathering of the following American principles and ideals.

They are of a political or social inclination and are randomly listed. Each is self-explanatory.

Peace (MN), Goodwill (WV), Loyal (OK), Congress (AZ), Court House (VA), Persist (OK), School (MN), Prospect (CA), Joy (TN), Hero (VT), Equality (WA), Success (MO), Trading (KS), Hope (MN), Service (OR), Charity (KY), Welcome (TX), Safety (NH), Strong (MA), Beautiful (NM), Discovery (WA), Industry (ME).

Besides the numerous factors that have contributed to a national and ethnographic consensus in America's toponomy, it has been concluded that domestic circumstances have also played a significant role. As one who traverses the country, blatant advertisements and promotional signs can be seen that reveal the merits of a particular food found at a nearby restaurant or farm. They usually expose specialties of the region.

One can readily enjoy Philadelphia cheese steaks, Maryland crabs, New Jersey tomatoes, Michigan cranberries, California wines, Southern fried chicken and Boston beans. Additionally, consumers can purchase New Mexico's tacos, Wisconsin cheese, Kentucky whiskey, New Haven pizza, Idaho potatoes, Vermont maple syrup, Washington apples, Rocky Mountain beer, Texas steaks, Maine lobster and Nebraska corncob. Each is commensurate with local resources and culinary tastes albeit they are thought to be national "treasures" as well.

The Alamo

an old mission at San Antonio, Texas

Alabama (AL)

From the name of an Indian tribe, a subdivision of the Creeks. Often spelled Alibamn or as known to the French as Alibamons.

Nicknames: Yellow hammer state and Heart of Dixie.

Arizona (AZ)

Probably from the Pima or Papago for "place of small springs". Some sources say the word means arid zone or desert, others claim it is an Aztec name signifying "Silver bearing".

Nickname: Grand Canyon State.

Arkansas (AR)

From term for Quapaw tribe given by other Indians. The village Arkansea was recorded in a French context as of 1675.

Nickname: Land of Opportunity.

California (CA)

Probably from the mythical island in Garcia Ordonez de Montalvo's 16th century "The Deeds of Esplandian," perhaps influenced by the word "calif," and the Spanish city "Cahorra".

Nickname: Golden State.

Colorado (CO)

From Spanish for the color red pertaining to the reddish river, a part of which rose in the territory now known as the Colorado River. The site's name of Colorado was sanctioned by Congress in 1861.

Nickname: Centennial State.

Connecticut (CT)

From the Mohican Indian word meaning "beside the long tidal river" or another interpretation is "without end river".

Nickname: Constitution State and Meeting State.

Delaware (DE)

For Thomas West, Lord De La Warr, colonial governor of Virginia, 1610-1611.

Nickname: First State and Diamond State.

Florida (FL)

Named by Juan Ponce de Leon for Pascua Florida (Easter festival of the flowers) his Spanish led discovery on Palm Sunday.

Nickname: Sunshine State.

Georgia (GA)

For King George II of England, 1732. Hernando de Soto explored the region in 1540.

Nicknames: Empire State of the South and Peach State.

Idaho (ID)

Name means "gem of the mountains". The Kiowa – Apache name for the well known Indian tribe in the greater region.

Nickname: Gem State.

Illinois (IL)

Corruption of "iliniwek (tribe of the Superior Men") with a French suffix meaning "band of men".

Nickname: Prairie State.

Indiana (IN)

For the land of Indians found by early settlers, discovering many distinct tribes living in the region. A company of traders bought the land from the Indians.

Nickname: Hoosier State.

Iowa (IA)

A tribal name recorded on a French map, in the vicinity of the Iowa River, as of 1673. The state's name was shortened from the tribal name of Ouaouia? to Iowa. Some think it implies "sleepy ones".

Nickname: Hawkeye State.

Kansas (KS)

Name: for Kansa or Kaw, "people of the south wind". Known to the Spaniards as Escansaque and the French as Kansa from 1673.

Nickname: Sunflower State. It was possibly referred to as "kanosas" a Sioux word for willow.

Kentucky (KY)

Name: Corruption of the Iroquois "kenta-ke (island of tomorrow) and meadow-land". It may also mean "dark and bloody ground or the prairies", in Indian parlance.

Nickname: Bluegrass State.

Louisiana (LA)

Name: For King Louis XIV by La Salle in 1681 in a French context.

Nickname: Pelican State.

Maine (ME)

Name: Either for Maine a province in France, or to distinguish mainland from islands in the Gulf of Maine. The fishermen, early on, referred to the region as the "Mayn" land.

Nickname: The Pine Tree State.

Maryland (MD)

For Henrietta Maria, queen consort of Charles I.

Nicknames: Colony was designed for Catholics. Old Line State, Free State.

Massachusetts (MA)

Name: For area tribe known as Massachuset whose name means "at or about the great hill," originally the name of a village recorded in 1616.

Nickname: Bay State.

Michigan (MI)

From the Fox mesikarni, "large lake." Some attribute the name to a "place to catch fish."

Nickname: Wolverine State.

Minnesota (MN)

Name: From the Sioux minisota, "sky-tinted waters". Or Minesota, Minnaysoto, or "water cloudy," or "much water."

Nickname: North Star State and Gopher State, Land of 10,000 Lakes.

Mississippi (MS)

Name: From the Ojibioa "misi sipi," "great river" or "gathering of all waters."

Nickname: Magnolia State.

Missouri (MO)

Name: From the llinwek Missouri "owner of big canoes" or from the Fox name, living at the mouth of the river or from the Indian reference to "muddy water".

Nickname: Show Me State.

Montana (MT)

Name: From Spanish Montana, "mountainous." In 1858 used as a name for a town during Pikes Peak gold region.

Nicknames: Treasure State and "Big Sky Country".

Nebraska (NB)

Name: From the Oto nebratha, "flat or shallow water," thus meaning a river not running between high banks, referring to the Platte River.
Nickname: Cornhusker State.

Nevada (NV)

Name: From Spanish meaning "snow covered sierra".
Nicknames: Sagebrush State and Silver State.

New Hampshire (NH)

Name: For English county of Hampshire in 1629.
Nickname: Granite State.

New Jersey (NJ)

Name: After English Channel Island of Jersey in a land grant to Sir George Carteret, who named it for his home off the coast of England.
Nickname: Garden State.

New Mexico (NM)

Name: After Spanish explorers in 1562, hopefully thinking that the discovery would be as rich as the original Mexico to the south.
Nickname: Land of Enchantment.

New York (NY)

Name: For Duke of York of England. Taken over from the Dutch city of Nieuw-Amsterdam in 1664, a reference to York in England.
Nickname: Empire State.

North Carolina (NC)

Name: For Charles II of England (Carolus is Latin for Charles) in 1629. The French colonists in 1564 used la Caroline for a fort on the coast.
Nicknames: Tarheel State and Old North State.

North Dakota (ND)

Name: A Sioux word for "allies" of the tribes from the northern section of the Dakota Territory, called "dakota".

Nicknames: Sioux State, Peace Garden State, Flickertail State.

Ohio (OH)

Name: From the Iroquois oleo, "beautiful, fine, good, attributing" it to the French modification applying it to the part of the river now known as Allegheny.

Nickname: Buckeye State.

Oklahoma (OK)

From the Choctaw Indians, "okla humma", land of the red people, the name was adopted in 1866, it also may mean "home for all Indians."

Nickname: Sooner State.

Oregon (OR)

Name: Its name is of unknown origin, but may have been a mistake on a French map of 1715, later referred to as Ouaricon, then Ourigan after the discovery of the Columbia River in 1778.

Nickname: Beaver State.

Pennsylvania (PA)

Name: For Admiral William Penn, father of its founder William Penn (a Welsh name meaning head land) by King Charles II. Sylva, a Latin word meaning forest, was added to the ending.

Nickname: Keystone State.

Rhode Island (RI)

Name: For the Mediterranean island of Rhodes. Situated in Narragansett Bay, a site for the followers of Roger Williams, who found sanctuary there from the religious restrictions practiced elsewhere.

Nicknames: Ocean State, Little Rhody.

South Carolina (SC)

Name: For King Charles II, a separate region from its northern neighbor North Carolina, it entered the Union in 1788. It was first named for Charles IX of France.

Nickname: Palmetto State.

South Dakota (SD)

Name: For southern section of Dakota Territory, like its neighbor to the north the name is derived from the Sioux term "allies". Dakota's South was applied to the territory by Congress in 1861.

Nicknames: Coyote State, Mount Rushmore State

Tennessee (TN)

Name: For Tenase, the principal village of the Cherokees. It may have been an Indian word meaning "cured spoon". The name was accepted by Congress in 1796 when Tennessee entered the Union.

Nickname: Volunteer State.

Texas (TX)

Name: From the Indians known as Teyas, as recorded on Spanish records as early as 1541. It was thought to mean "friends," later regarded as "the great kingdom of Texas." It was deemed to receive an official designation under Spain and Mexico.

Nickname: Lone Star State.

Utah (UT)

Name: From the Ute or Uta Indians, meaning home on the mountaintop. Brighman Young, a Mormon leader led his people to the Salt Lake Valley in 1847.

Nicknames: Beehive State, Mormon State.

Vermont (VT)

Name: From French "vert mont" or "green mountain", a name officially adopted in 1777.

Nickname: Green Mountain State.

Virginia (VA)

Name: Named for Elizabeth I, called the Virgin Queen. The first successful English settlement was in Virginia, at Jamestown in 1607.

Nicknames: Old Dominion, Mother of Presidents, Mother of States.

Washington (WA)

Name: For George Washington, a state named by Congress in 1853, in honor of the President. Many places bear the name.

Nickname: Evergreen State.

West Virginia (WV)

Name: for the western part of Virginia. At the time of the organization of the new state in 1862 after three other names were rejected at a convention, after that part of the state had not joined the Confederacy.

Nickname: Mountain State

Wisconsin (WI)

Name: From the Ojibwa "wishkonsing, place of the bearer," as of 1673 recorded in French as Mecousing and Mesconsing, possibly named for a river within the present Wisconsin.

Nickname: Badger State

Wyoming (WY)

Name: From the Delaware "manugh-wau-wa-ma, or "large plains", or mountains and valleys alternating", a term applied to a region of Pennsylvania.

Nickname: Equality State

City Nicknames

1. Windy City (Chicago)
2. Motown (Detroit)
3. Big Apple (New York City)
4. Big Easy (New Orleans)
5. Bean Town (Boston)
6. Sin City (Las Vegas)
7. City of Brotherly Love (Philadelphia)
8. Mile High City (Denver)
9. Tinsel Town and City of Angels (Los Angeles)
10. Twin Cities (St. Paul/Minneapolis)
11. Steel City (Pittsburgh)
12. City of Roses (Portland)
13. Crossroads of America (Indianapolis)
14. Gateway to the Goldfields (Sacramento)
15. Gateway to the South (Louisville)

William Penn

Benjamin Franklin

VII.

~

NAMES HAVING LITERARY INFLUENCES

Anthropologists dealing with the scientific investigations of man's origin, and their later movements of the migrations of people from place to place, often had to face uncertainties in their retelling of folk ways. The etymology of a word and its early primary origins, at times proved to be confusing. This task was extremely burdensome when it came to hypothesizing, or accurately pinpointing precise locations. Dead languages had to be dealt with. Therefore, in time, when written accounts came into being, the validity of a place-name's beginnings evolved. Many became apparent when surroundings came to the fore. The relationship between the geography and the underlying dynamics of toponomy commenced. Holding to true conceptualizing, the merger of man and map naming terms endure, as do speculating about a wide spectrum of fantasies.

In the 18th and 19th centuries the history of the United States manifested many kinds of controversial issues confronting national leaders in politics, religion and journalism. Questions about freedom, independence, state's rights and the staggering matter of ways to deal with slavery were in the fore of all other considerations. The excessive writings of opinions foment fierce debates between divergent segments of the populace.

A consequence of the outpouring vehemently expressed in pamphlets, journal articles and books led to bitter feelings accentuated by vested economic interests and long-standing sectionalism. In some quarters vengeance and retributions ruled the day.

Though unrelated, a somewhat similar scenario of events were taking place in Italy with its citizenry being aroused by the unification-motivations of the collection of provinces. There the diatribes and rantings pitted the "sword" (military), the "tongue" (orator) and the "pen" (writer) against each other. With the pen, printed materials were able to reach a larger audience with their message. Thus the writers, with the power of the pen, eventually won out, and Italy became unified as a nation. Apparently their literary influences had spoken.

In the United States, it seems, politics and literary endeavors seemed to have been integrated into one voice. That was inherent since the country's beginnings. Samuel Adams and Benjamin Franklin used their writings to stress the need for forming a new government.

In the Federalist, a series of 85 essays published in 1787/88 urged the reader to consider the virtues of writing a new constitution for which Alexander Hamilton and James Madison received credit. Their works became a classic statement of American governmental theory. Thomas Jefferson was instrumental in the writing of the Declaration of Independence. His papers argued for individual freedom and self-governing at the local level. Autonomy was to accompany decentralization. The will to enact strong laws by Congress for uniformity in its constituencies has been deliberated since time immemorial. The influence of writers has historically been quite significant.

Alexander Hamilton opposed the philosophy of Jefferson. He wrote that there was a great need for a strong centralized government. Jefferson's writing prompted Andrew Jackson's beliefs in a true democracy. Each of these earlier founding politicians have had numerous places named for them in honor of their service to their country.

Oratorical and literary luminaries of the past ushered in interesting verse, novels and biographies for American homes and libraries. Outstanding writers of fiction and non-fiction books included Charles Dickens, John Quincy Adams, Washington Irving, Henry Clay, Davy Crockett and Daniel Webster. Also, contributing to the aforementioned were such poets and writers as William Jennings Bryant and Ralph Waldo Emerson with their writing products. Creative projects was their forte. A check of any atlas will indicate that these figures have permeated maps with the remembrances of their names, all representing a kind of literary Hall of Fame.

Two famous writings of Abraham Lincoln served as cornerstones of American democracy. His Emancipation Proclamation (January 1, 1869) in which he underscored the need to bring about the end of slavery and the Gettysburg Address (May 1863), an incisive declaration that "all men are created equal".

Place-named after the aforementioned writers appear in the states of South Dakota, Nebraska, Washington, New Jersey, Texas, Iowa and Massachusetts. Ralph Waldo Emerson is also the name of a place in New Jersey. Lord Byron (NY), and Benjamin Franklin (PA) are writers that have been honored too. In the state of Washington, Booker T. Washington, a former black slave, has a place-name of Booker as a remembrance of a dozen books he wrote, some being translated into more than 18 languages.

Additional authors, perhaps because of their controversial abolitionist anti-slavery views, have only a dearth of names placed in their memory.

Francis Scott Key wrote "The Star Spangled Banner" while on a prison ship in Baltimore harbor in 1814. It eventually became the lyrics of the American National anthem. In another harbor (NY), Emma Lazarus wrote the most inspiring message of hope inscribed on the Statue of Liberty; dedicated on October 28, 1886.

George Washington

Thomas Jefferson

James Madison

James Monroe

JOHN QUINCY ADAMS

HENRY CLAY

VIII.

~

NAMES OF UNKNOWN BEGINNINGS

Expressions and tales passed on from generation to generation may acquire a certain regional or ethnic tone. Their styles can be relegated to the name pronunciations of places, which can readily be twisted or distorted when conversing with others. That can result in map misnomers over time. The early origins of places named on maps may be a consequence of exaggerations or illusions stemming from passing along oral folk legends. Historically, most likely they were of unknown origins and therefore be of limited use for toponomy detectives. Also, valid information was lost to the passing of time.

The folklore invariably stressed traditional beliefs, legends, sayings and customs of people whose lives were impacted by their area's geographic conditions. It was not uncommon to reap coined or fabricated names from the oft repeated tales. Many of the place-name vocabulary were ultimately accepted as truisms, only to appear on later maps, confounding toponym investigators and cartographers.

Informal polls of geographers, historians, teachers and the governmental officials of a place are often unable to account for the name genesis of surroundings that play significant roles in their lives. It is not uncommon to encounter people who do not even know the origin of their own names.

There are hundreds of place-names, according to Stewart and Gannett, toponymers, in which place-names are of unknown origin. It is thought that a number of place-name beginnings are clouded, or lack authenticity. The mysteries about them are attributed to different reasons. Some of them are conjecture in nature. Some are sheer folly. Rationales abound. These include: Early names that have had misnomers or alterations. Original names that were once disliked and dismissed. There was overlapping of foreign words with Indian language terminology. And pioneers, frontiersmen and avant-gardes sometimes found a new tract to be so useless or unattractive that they shied away from naming it, no matter what.

IX.

~

POSSESSIVE AND PERSONAL NAMES

A personal name consists of a given name and a full surname upon which is known or addressed. The latter may be from an ancestral line of descent going back for centuries. A first name can be selected from hundreds of possibilities, some amongst which are often timely and popular. Once a place-name is affixed onto a map it can be removed in order to satisfy the unfolding of current or historical events. That is what happened when the Soviet Union collapsed and previous place-names were restored. The physical transformation or alteration of a landscape may also dictate name changes.

Legal titles assuring possession and accompanying rights can be obtained in a number of ways. Documents must show name clarity and absolute listing of acquisition data. Primogeniture, in which the eldest son has the exclusive right to his father's estate, may be written into the family's deed.

Over the years people, churches and other institutions have been awarded land grants and huge tracts of land through Congressional offerings. The territories had a sundry array of place-names reflecting terrain, purchases and treaties with the many tribes of Native Americans. Today land grant colleges bear the names of the United State's government foresight and educational planning.

In the years following the allocation of the lands by governmental bureaus to private ownership, descriptive place-names, many of which reflected the propietorship's own names appeared on newly drawn maps. All over the expanse of lands by railroad builders, fortune seekers, ranchers, farmers and miners "opened the wild west". Missionaries and religious zealots led to the assignment of appropriate place-names to their discoveries and land claims as well.

Possessive names are those that indicate a particular ownership of some sort. Places are named for landholders and settlers, or obviously for a site's original owner or founder. A name might include a title of office.

In the commercial world, where there is a need for repeat business, it is imperative that customers require a familiarization with a place. Advertisements are paramount. Professional services integrate a personal name with the provider's background and the specialization being rendered.

Possessive names can be eclectic and far-reaching. They may refer to descriptive adjectives and nouns that make inferences about a place. Such examples like Florida's climate, Arizona's arid deserts, San Francisco's fog or Pennsylvania's Donora's pollution stand out. A recall of American history tells us about the Indian fighter, Colonel Custer's last stand in the infamous battle that took place near the Little Big Horn River in southern Montana in 1876.

The majority of place-names can be traced back to family names, given names, and from nicknames. Family names delineated on maps arise from multiple sources, albeit primarily from ancestral lines of descent. Personal names tend to be endearing, or often in memory of a departed person's involvement with an incident that may have taken place at a site dear to the occupant's heart. The application of personal names, may turn out to be rather colorful since they may be transformed from original Indian idioms. At any rate, personal name identifications on maps have proven to be the most prolific of all imparted, or in everyday references in conversations.

The United States, at mid 19th century, saw the birth of a slew of railroads and the accompanying naming of junctions and railway stations. The country then became much more accessible for trade and travel, especially after the completion of the transcontinental railroad at Promontory Point, Utah in 1869, linking east and west. A golden spike was driven into the track there in celebration of the laborious task which took years to accomplish.

In the colorful saga of the "wild west," sheriffs and judges had to rely on the maxim that "possession is nine-tenths of the law," when settling disputes over land ownership cases. That aphorism is best played out over conflicts – even gun battles between factions claiming land rights. Entering into the fray were squatters, Native Americans, ranchers, farmers, sheep herders, miners and railroad builders. The matter of entitlements triggered the upheaval. Personal and possessive names overlapped. A bitter family feud between the Hatfields and Mc Coys, antagonists, over land, lasted for years, with confrontations spread near and far.

Personal and possessive names assured the titles of such intriguing and diverse categories as animals, incidents, geographic phenomenon and even curious nicknames. Within that list one can find Ice's Ferry (WV), Jacob's Well (AZ), Bakersfield (CA), Pike's Peak (CO), Seward's Folly (NB), Penns Grove (NJ), Sisters Peak (OR) and Steamboat Springs (MO). There is a Lake Ida (FL), Helen's Mountain (MT), Lawrenceville (NJ) and Marysville (CA). Sutters Mill (CA) is where gold was discovered and the description of Skunks Nursery (NY) speaks for itself, as do Bee (TX), Bear Creek (CA) and Beer Gulch (CA).

Note: The possessive form showing ownership in grammatical expressions used in this text relied on the adjectives guiding inquires of "which one, what kind, how many?"

Colonel G. A. Custer

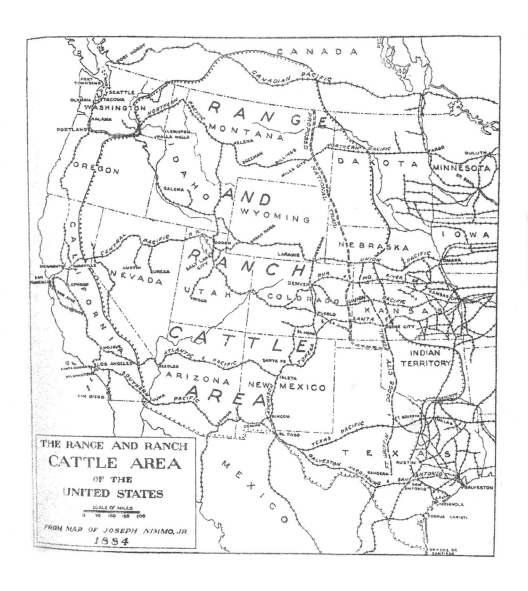

X.

RELIGIOUS AND MYTHICAL NAMES

During and after the early sixteen hundreds religious problems increased under the rule of the English monarchs. Substantial groups of discontented church members set out for the new world, departing their mother country seeking self-determination and freedom to worship in ways of their choice. They had visions of opportunities unavailable in their native towns and villages. Many became outcasts, willing to endure the hardships of a trans Atlantic Ocean voyage, and the unknowns of coping with the climate, crop growing and unfriendly Native Americans who might prove to be hostile to them.

Upon their arrival in New England, Virginia and elsewhere, they refused to forget their past. Consequently, they were quite agreeable to the proposition that their new settlements assume similar place-names as found back in England. Also royalty, especially those dispensing charters for their new colonies, were rewarded with having places named in their honor.

As the English began to find and farm the coastal areas along the seaboard, east of the Allegheny Mountains, they strengthened their lot by establishing footholds before venturing through the passes to the fertile basins beyond. The French, on the other hand, spread out throughout North America seeking riches by fur-trapping and trading pelts with

Native peoples. They frequented many river banks in their quests for animal furs, which were in great demand in Europe at that time.

Spaniards in the new world were bent on establishing Catholic missions and finding gold, periodically returning to Spain with their gold treasures. Though except for a few missions in California and the Southwest they too spread their outposts and settlements sparsely. Their outcomes in converting Native Americans to Christianity were reasonably successful, but major inroads were made with the introduction of the Spanish language throughout America.

A perusal of United States maps will show numerous place-names and geographic terms infused by long-standing French and Spanish toponyms. Each name on the map offers enriching information about their cultures and their name derivations. Deciphering place-names is a worthy challenge and stimulating mental exercise for the curious and all wanting to obtain enriching expositions about American history – in particular about the contributions of the immigrants of previous generations. The how and why they selected certain place-names. A toponomy for the times.

The phrase "where did this name come from" can now be readily answered.

A priority for the earliest Protestant settlers in the New World was the building of a church. Sites were often chosen on top of a hill in order to ward off potential Indian attacks from below. In time the Christian sects moved down into the valleys and lowlands where they were able to practice their strict religious beliefs with immunity. Since many worshipers were unable to read or write they were easily swayed by the sermons of their ministers in the explanations of the need to pray and obey the will of God and most certainly to keep the faith. Bible teachings about good and evil and salvation were constantly being preached.

Over the years, as the English speaking immigrants and others increased, and moved to locations within the interior of the United States. They most often carried the Bible with them. It served them well as an uplifting guide, especially in the newest of frontiers. As the religious communities established their new habitations they sought out appropriate names for them. They affectionately turned to the Bible. Therefore, names like Salem, Bethlehem, Bethel and Bethesda came into being, derived from the holy book.

French and Spanish locations tended to recognize their own native explorers and missionaries in selecting names for certain land claims in the United States. Names bestowed included prefixes such as Saint and San, in tribute to their Catholic heritages and patrons. Saint Louis and San Diego, names of prominent cities in the United States, is each set for posterity.

Any number of Americans became aroused by reading about stories in mythology. The fictitious accounts were quite intriguing. They focused on their own interpretations of gods and heroes like Hercules, renowned for his superhuman strength. The inspirations to read and fanaticize about imagined people and places possibly came from witches and soothsayers who mysteriously claimed to have the ability to shed light on the origin of man. These atypical individuals fabricated and spread much about myths and its related terminology. Consequently, some of the places named in the lexicon of the titles of United States toponyms, may have revealed curious sources and birthplaces. Their names have remained truly unique.

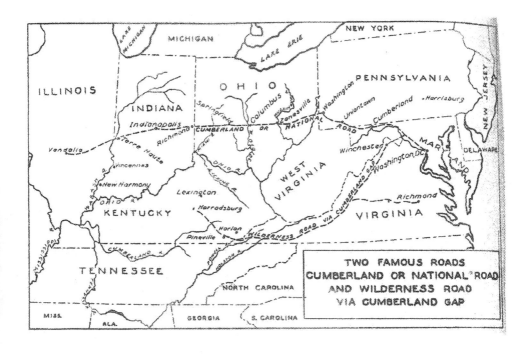

TWO FAMOUS ROADS
CUMBERLAND OR NATIONAL ROAD
AND WILDERNESS ROAD
VIA CUMBERLAND GAP

THE GREAT PLAINS AND BORDERING REGIONS

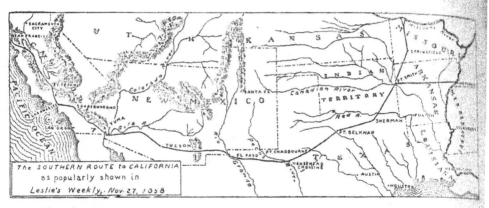

The SOUTHERN ROUTE to CALIFORNIA as popularly shown in Leslie's Weekly, Nov. 27, 1858

Popular interest in Western routes during and after the gold rush led to the publication of maps in many magazines and newspapers. This is a facsimile of a map extending across the top half of two pages of *Leslie's Weekly* for November 27, 1858.

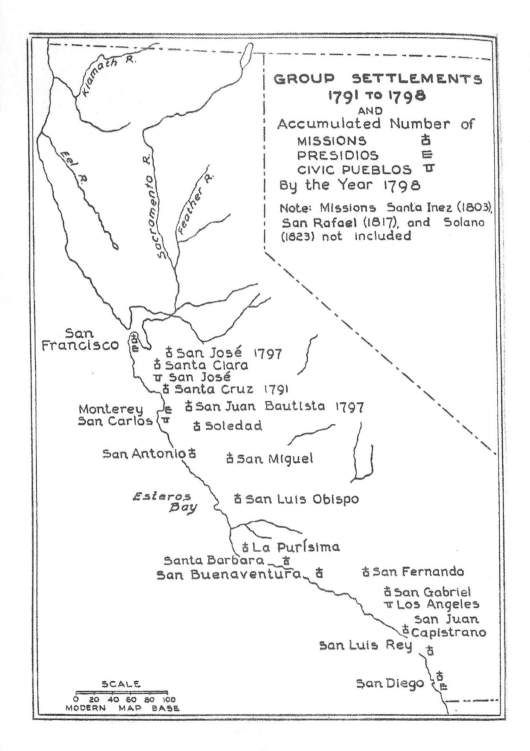

GROUP SETTLEMENTS
1791 TO 1798
AND
Accumulated Number of
MISSIONS   ⚕
PRESIDIOS   E
CIVIC PUEBLOS   ⊔
By the Year 1798

Note: Missions Santa Inez (1803),
San Rafael (1817), and Solano
(1823) not included

Klamath R.

Eel R.

Sacramento R.

Feather R.

San Francisco

⚕San José 1797
⚕Santa Clara
⊔San José
⚕Santa Cruz 1791
⚕San Juan Bautista 1797
Monterey
San Carlos
⚕Soledad

San Antonio⚕   ⚕San Miguel

Esteros Bay   ⚕San Luis Obispo

⚕La Purísima
Santa Barbara
San Buenaventura   ⚕   ⚕San Fernando

⚕San Gabriel
⊔Los Angeles
San Juan
Capistrano
San Luis Rey

San Diego

SCALE
0 20 40 60 80 100
MODERN MAP BASE

The initial religious fervor in North America took hold when Spanish conquistadors planted their national flag on present-day St. Augustine, Florida, in 1565. Later they and French explorers, along with friars and priests, built missions throughout undeveloped, sparsely settled locations. An underlying purpose of their endeavors was to imbue Native Americans with their brand of religion and faith.

In the early centuries of United States history thousands of Scots, Irish, French and Germans, as well as English Puritans came to the "new world" in order to flee unacceptable religious doctrines and practices prevalent in Europe at that time. Though there was much religious diversity amongst the newcomers there was a common embrace of the Bible. Ultimately that interest and familiarity led to the naming of hundreds of habitations and natural features, either directly or indirectly, after Biblical sites or incidents.

A representative list, using full or partial names and places within certain states follows:

Place-names having Biblical connotations

Abilene (KS), Antioch (CA), Ararat (CA), Baptist (KY), Bashan (CT), Beersheba (TN), Bethany (CT), Bethlehem (PA), Canaan (CT), Cathedral (CA), Christmas (OR), Dothan (AL), Egypt (TX), Emmaus (PA), Ephrata (PA), Goshen (IN), Heaven (AL), Hebron (CT), Jerusalem (OH), Jordan (VT), Judea (AR), Lebanon (CT), New Ark (NJ), Palestine (TN), Preacher (OR), Providence (RI), Sodom (NY), Solomon (CO), Zion (VT), Zoar (OH).

Place-names having Spanish saints remembered. Fifty missions were built in California by early missionaries. These names remain:

Corpus Christi (TX), San Antonio (TX), San Bernardino, San Diego, San Francisco, San Joaquin, San Jose, San Luis Obispo, San Pedro, Santa Anna, Santa Barbara, Santa Clara, Santa Cruz, Santa Monica, Santa Rosa (All in CA).

XI.

MANUFACTURED AND CONTRIVED NAMES

C ontrived words are usually devised or "manufactured". The place-names that are "invented" are mostly of a rather recent vintage, often designed around local land features and environmental characteristics that play a significant role in the promotion of an area. The artificial name selections tend, at times, to offer attractive incentives for people and industries from other localities to relocate there.

The new places can be planned and realized through the annexation of adjoining land sites, by large scale home building on undeveloped acreage, by merging with other previously established municipalities, by the expansion of existing plants, warehouses and institutions and by the further development of nearby natural resources. Manufactured names are formed with a particular promotional purpose, complying with a need to match the name with its appeal for tourism, as a beneficial health resort, as a park-land, military base or science center. The made-up epithet, more than likely, is designed to comply with special nearby geographic surroundings or a famous rage of the past.

Following the termination of World War II the United States experience radical changes in its man-made landscapes. New ventures of intermixing educational and recreational sites were undertaken. Ribbon cutting ceremonies recognized outstanding names in literature, science, entertainment, politics, sports and ethnic groups, by attributing place-names to their manifold contributions. The NASA Space Center at Cape Canaveral, Florida and the Disney World theme parks in and around Orlando, Florida are examples that warranted special tributes. So too did the one in Anaheim, California.

Recreational theme parks, with their commercially oriented complexes, sprung up, seemingly out of nowhere. The new type developments proved to be magnets for people and businesses. They also were given credit for major improvements in land and air transportation with the construction of airports and interstate highways. The naming of such popular air hubs as JFK, for America's fallen president and dissimilar naming of roadside rest stops after local heroes, Vince Lombardi, football coach, and Joyce Kilmer, famous New Jersey poet-author were designed for the 21st century traveler's needs in mind. Sun City in California, and a whole host of new enterprising sites like condominiums, were built with the longer-living retirees in the builders' marketing sights being first and foremost.

In the state of Florida there was a boom in attracting tourists and others to such beach resort towns as Miami, Daytona, Vero, Palm, Boynton and Fort Meyers. To augment those sites there suddenly appeared a rash of Indian sponsored gambling casinos like the Seminoles in Florida and the Mohicans in Connecticut. They too took on the names of local tribes of past days, like many others did throughout the country.

XII.

~

HUMOROUS INCIDENTS
AND ODD NAMES

Over the years Americans have demonstrated a propensity for creating humorous names for places based on some incident or an unexpected experience at sites. The funny encounter or outcome can be witty, leaving an everlasting place-name associated with it. Such episodes are sometimes embellished by others during comical routines meant to mildly denigrate the place-name in order to get laughs from an audience. Some of the place-name's caricature may take hold, even appearing on maps in due time. They may also reflect favorably on America's sense of humor.

Odd names permeate throughout the United States. Oddities are most often associated with the actions of eccentric individuals and/or peculiar places. The "strange" labels affixed to place-names can be carried forth for decades. They may also be transferred from, or be an offshoot of unfounded stereotypes which can focus on people, geographic phenomenon, animals or local stories which tend to be colorful, yet fictitious, even morbid or ghostly.

Nicknames and creative humor are inherent in describing America's personality, past and present.

It is said that American humor started around western campfires with exaggerated retelling of incidents encountered with Native Americans.

127

They most often included scenarios about places where new immigrants resided, with stereotypes and degradations.

Political cartoons highlighted current values and conflicts. Ralph Waldo Emerson, the famous American writer said that "Caricatures are often the truest history of the times". Benjamin Franklin, the father of the American political cartoon drew the famous "Join or Die", in 1754. Later the U.S. was inundated with clever cartoons featured in print journals and used as weapons against corrupt politicians. The most striking cartoon of its day was the appeal to voters in the 1840 election to cast their vote for "Tippecanoe (IN) and Tyler too".

Will Rogers (1879-1935) part Native American and Oklahoma cowboy made jokes about American society. He was regarded as America's humorist, declaring "The day is lost when one has not laughed".

Invariably it seems, later on, "stand-up" comedians loved to poke fun, rather light-handedly, about funny sounding place-names. Included in their material were Walla Walla (WA), Kokomo (IN), Hoboken (NJ), Schenectady (NY), Yum Yum (TN), Yucca (AZ) and Nunathloogagamiutbingoi (AK), the longest place-name in the country happens to be in Alaska and that's a cold fact.

Humorous, odd and incident names tend to develop from an imaginary set of circumstances, including the nature of the event, its location and impressions by the name providers. Their quickly formulated impressions may be lasting when bestowing a name upon a place. Their views may be interpreted in the "eyes of the beholder" and carried on to others when making a reference to a place. Intermingling of the three discrete factors may come into play with an overlapping lexicon resulting.

Partial or complete words consisting of an array
of odd US place-name term origins:

Alarm Clock (TX):   Because a party of surveyors who were camped here promised to give the settlers an alarm in case of an Indian incursion.

Baldy (MT):   A generic term for mountain tops bare of trees.

Boca Raton (FL):   City in South Florida meaning mouth of the rat.

Bogus (CA):   A name common in mining districts where counterfeiters once operated.

Boneyard (AZ):   Where places showed evidence of starved cattle due to a deep snow.

Bottle (WY):   A whiskey bottle atop a mountain named for its shape.

Calamity (TX):   Where people were drowned in a flood.

Cannibal (CO):   Scene of a killing of five companions for subsistence during the winter of 1873-1874, by eating parts of their bodies.

Cash (SD):   For Casius Timmons, an early rancher.

Chocolate (AZ):   A description of brown colored mountains.

Coffin Rock (OR):   Indians used this spot to deposit their dead in canoes.

Cripple Creek (OR):   A stream in Oregon named for a surveyor who cut his foot there with an ax.

Cutthroat (CA):   The gulch where a Chinese miner was discovered there in 1860 with his throat cut.

Death (CA):   A barren and hostile region that attributed to the death of a party of immigrants due to thirst and starvation.

Deposit (NY):	Named so for former lumber deposits.
Difficulty (VA):	A stream hard to cross or to follow.
Disappointment(WA):	By an English explorer unable to find a river mouth there.
Dismal (NC):	So named because of the dismal appearance of a swamp.
Doubling (WY):	A description of a variety of natural features like springs, mountain, bayou and run (stream) at that site.
Fairplay (CO):	Established by gold miners as a response to their "grab-all" neighbors.
Feather (CA):	A river, translated from the early Spanish name, Plumas.
Fear (NC):	Cape and river named for a sailor who narrowly escaped being wrecked there due to a wicked storm.
Flathead (MT):	Named for an Indian tribe, by early settlers, who had a custom of flattening the heads of infants on a board.
Frying Pan (WY):	A name suggestive of heat used for a thermal spring.
Gallows Hill (NJ):	Was the scene of a hanging and burning at the stake in 1717.
Gin Creek (VA):	Probably from the presence of a cotton gin.
Grandfather (NC):	From an association with a "great stone face" or old man in appearance on a mountain-side.
Graveyard (AZ):	Two men, brutally killed in a frontier feud, were left unburied for many days, until interred in one grave.
Gunsight (AZ):	An upstanding rock resembling a gun barrel.

Gypsy (OK):   A woman's name, and the name of an oil company.

Hangman (SD):   Site where three horse thieves were hanged in early days.

Headache Springs (CA):   Supposedly drinking from the springs caused headaches.

Hobo (CA):   Informal indictment against some itinerant workmen for alleged misconduct on a neighbor's farm.

Kidney (UT):   A descriptive shape of a lake.

Kill (NY):   Derived from Indian, Dutch and incident applications.

Kiss Me Quick (SD):   Referred to forewarnings of road bumps ahead.

Lost (ID):   A widespread term denoting various nouns such as rivers, people and inexplicable equipment at a number of sites.

Man (CA):   An expression about a "man cow," or bull, chasing a young lady.

Mother (NB):   For a large lake in the midst of smaller ones.

Needmore (KY):   A common usage in Kentucky and elsewhere implying that the place needs more of everything.

No Man's Friend (GA):   A pond named in a hostile area of swamps and thickets.

Old Woman (CA):   Mountains in CA perceived as a stereotype in its referral.

Poverty (CA):   Named for an unproductive hill where gold findings were nil.

Purgatory (WV):   Of Protestant origin; a peak in WV with its rough and rather insurmountable nature.

Sand Pudding (NB): A cowboy encampment had sand blown into their pudding.

Sleepy Eye (MN): Lake and village named for an Indian chief whose eyes had the appearance of sleep.

Smackover (AR): From a French word meaning stream or road covered over.

Smuggler (ND): Point of entry of illicit trade from Canada.

Spoon (IL): From "mussel shell" because Indians used them as spoons.

Stink (OR): Because the name is applied by the strong smell from sulphur compounds stemming from nearby waters.

Superstition (AZ): From local Indian lore associating local mountains with supernatural happenings.

Surprise (CA): A valley where conastoga wagon emigrants were startled to see much lower terrain, a valley beyond the heights.

Thief (OR): A valley where a mule-stealer was hanged there in 1864.

Tin Cup (CO): A story that claimed the first gold found in the area was in gravel scooped with a tin cup.

Tippecanoe (IN): River village, and county for an Indian word meaning "at the great clearing," and "buffalo fish".

Tombstone (AZ): Prior to exploring a mine it was predicted that because of the threat from the Apaches it would lead to the miner's tombstone.

Tongue (OR): Named in 1792 for a projecting tongue of land.

Truth (NY): A commendatory name as given as Truthville early on.

Witch (AZ):	A translation from the Mohave tribe, believing the site was a place haunted by witches.
Yell (AZ):	Named for Col. Archibald Yell, killed at Buena Vista in 1847.

ENRICHING COMPILATIONS

Many faces from many places dotted the American landscape since their forebearers set forth upon the soils of their new land decades ago. Their backgrounds were diverse. Seeking freedom was commonplace. Their quest for a better life tended to be a motivation for the many that sailed away from troublesome events in their native countries. Some came to claim riches from uncharted territories, yet to be named.

Once, after explorations or settlements were established, identifications had to become an uppermost priority by the mapping of places found. Names were selected based on the whims and impulses of group leaders or others with ideas for place-naming. Many tended to voice their choices upon the environmental offerings exposed in the nearby whereabouts.

Fitting supplements designated to provide further insights are provided herewith: the wide range of topical headings assist in the organization of a whole slew of fascinating varieties of place-names and where they are located. Examples follow:

Animal: Moosehead (ME), Mustang Bayou (TX), Foxborough (MA), Snake River (ID), Antelope Creek (WY), Buffalo Leap (NB), Muleshoe (TX), Horse Creek (CO), Greybull (WY), Big Bear (CA), Bull Spring (SD), Deerfield (FL), Caribou (CO), Wolf Run (WV),

Color: Yellowstone National Park (WY), Red Bank (NJ), Greenbelt (MD), Red Cloud (NE), Greensboro (NC), Green Bay (WI), Greybull (WY),

Black Hills (SD), Blue Ridge Mountains (VA), Blackbeard's Point (NC), Silver Tip Creek (MT), White Cloud (MI)

Direction: North Bend (OR), East Stroudsburg (PA), North Platte (NE), West Point (NY), South Bend (IN), South Prairie (WA), Eastlawn (MI), Northridge (CA), East Orange (NJ), West Chester (PA), East Liverpool (OH)

Persons of Note: Douglas (GA), Elizabeth (NJ), Charleston (SC), Dewey (OK), Monroe (LA), Sam Rayburn Res (TX), Franklin (TX), Hamilton (OH), Jackson (MS), Jamesburg (NJ), Kearney (NJ), Houston (TX), Kosciusko (MS), Lafayette (LA), Louisburg (NC), Levy (FL), Jefferson City (MO), Jefferson Davis (GA), Buchanan (MO), Carnegie (PA), Edison (NJ),

Geographic: Klamath Falls (OR), Oyster Bayou (TX), Donner Pass (CA), Plainfield (NJ), Lakeland (FL), Little Falls (MN), Long Beach (NY), Key West (FL), Sand Pudding Lake (NB), Keyport (NJ), Sandy Hook (NJ), San Joaquin Valley (CA), Silver Spring (MD), Bluff (VT), Newport Beach (CA), Olive Hill (KY), Cape Girardeau (MO), Grand Rapids (MI), High Point (NC), Ocean City (MD), Riverside (CA), Mountain Home (SD), Mojave Desert (CA), Piedmont (MO), Summit (NJ), Divide (CO),

History: Gettysburg (PA), Bunker Hill (IL), Alamo Heights (TX), Harper's Ferry (WV), Morristown (NJ), Bennington (VT), Revere (MA), Jefferson City (MO), Johnstown (PA), Marion (SC), New Orleans (LA), Washington (DC), Valley Forge (PA), Pikes Peak (CO), Pontiac (MI), St. Augustine (FL), Drake (CA)

Incidents: Appomattox (VA), Gold Bluffs (CA), Liberty (NC), Lewis and Clark (OR), Lexington (MA), Death Valley (CA), Raleigh (NC), Plymouth (MA), Gadsden (AK), Titanic (OK), Tippecanoe (IN), Custer (MT), Gallows Hill (NJ), Garfield (NJ)